The Self-Publishing Road Map

RJ CRAYTON

DEDICATION

This book is dedicated to all the people out there who have a story to tell and want to put it out in the world through self-publishing.

CONTENTS

Introduction 1

Step 1: Determine Your Goals 3
Traditional Publishing vs. Self-Publishing
Step 1 Checklist

Step 2: Write Good Books 10
Write a Lot
Writing Habit
What to Write
Accountability for Your Work
Pseudonyms
A Note about Author Names
Beta Readers Improve Your Book
Timing the Release of Your Book
Step 2 Checklist

Step 3: Polishing to Professional 25
Editing
Covers
Book Description (Blurb)
Taglines
Step 3 Checklist

Step 4: Publish 38
Copyright Registration
Front & Back Matter Formatting
Banking, Emails
Digital Sales Channels
Formatting for Different Vendors
Distributors, Libraries & Subscription Services
Vendors to Distribute to Directly
Creating Vendor Accounts
Categories & Keywords
Digital Pricing
Pre-Orders
ISBNs & Other Book Identifiers
Creating Your Print Book
Lightning Source & Lulu
Getting Paid

Getting Into Bookstores and Libraries
Updating Your Book
Unpublishing
Step 4 Checklist
Step 5: Marketing 83
Website
Goodreads & Amazon Author Central
Reviews
Discount Advertising Sites
Free
Mailing Lists
Blogs
Social Media
Marketing Additional Pseudonyms
Holidays
Festivals, Public Events
Other Ideas
Step 5 Checklists
Step 6: Be Professional 122
Don't Respond to Reviews
Don't Gripe About Fans to your Fans
Don't Swap Reviews
Don't Talk Trash about Other Authors
Don't Miss Deadlines
Not All Authors are Above the Fray
Step 7: Collect Data, Assess 128
Book Sales
Expenses
Advertising
Success stories
Your Story 139
Appendices
Appendix A: Checklists 141
Appendix B: Service Providers 152
Appendix C: Acronym Cheat Sheet 157
Appendix D: Articles 158
Thank You 198
About the Author 199
Also By This Author 200

ACKNOWLEDGMENTS

I've had a wonderful time writing this book. However, I couldn't have written a word of it, if I hadn't spent the last year and a half self-publishing and meeting some wonderful people, who were willing to share their knowledge and expertise with me. I'd like to thank my buddy, Jim Brown, who keeps his finger on the pulse of everything that is self-publishing. I also want to thank my colleagues at Indies Unlimited, both past and present, who have taught me so, so much. They're a super caring, friendly and fun loving group that includes: Stephen Hise (the evil mastermind), KS Brooks, Al Kuntz, Laurie Boris, Carolyn Steele, Carol Wyer, Cathy Speight, Chris James, DV Berkom, Dick Waters, Jim DeVitt, Lois Lewandowski, Lynne Cantwell, Martin Crosbie, Melinda Clayton, Melissa Bowersock, Melissa Pearl, Shawn Inmon, TD McKinnon and Yvonne Hertzberger. Lastly, I want to thank the folks at the Mitchellville Writers Group. They are great beta readers (if you don't know what they are, betas are explained in Step 2). Specifically, I want to thank the people who read this book and offered invaluable feedback that improved it: Kimiko Lighty, Jim Brown, Tim Brown, Karen Minors, Josephus Perry, and Diane Williams.

Introduction

There are a multitude of books out there on self-publishing, and many of them claim to have methods to make you an overnight success or guarantee you earn thousands of dollars per month. This isn't one of those books. People can and do earn money self-publishing. However, self-publishing is not a get-rich-quick scheme. As a former reporter for a publication called *Solid Waste Report*, I can assure you that anyone who tells you self-publishing is a way to get rich quick is selling you a load of crap.

So, what is self-publishing success and what does it take to achieve it? Different writers are going to define success differently, but the key components include putting out a professional product that sells and finds a readership. If you follow these steps, you'll find that success. Will you become a millionaire? Well, how many people do you know who have become millionaires from writing books? How many people do you know who have become millionaires in general, regardless of their occupation? Given that the likelihood of becoming a millionaire in any field is on the slimmer side, let's look at what you can realistically expect. In terms of money, you should expect a steady stream of royalties on a monthly basis, with the amount increasing the more books you publish. On the nonmonetary side, expect to put out a good book.

Before we get too deep into the book, I should tell you a little bit about myself. I'm a former journalist who is now a self-published (or indie) author. As a journalist, I've worked for *The Wichita Eagle* and *Kansas City Star*, as well as several smaller publications. I embraced self-publishing midway through 2013, since then publishing seven books (two under a pseudonym). I'm a monthly contributor for the blog Indies Unlimited, voted by *Publishers Weekly* as one of the six top blogs for indie publishers. There, we practice, write about, and see the entire spectrum of self-publishing success and failure, so I've learned a lot about the process. The key thing I've learned is that anyone can have self-publishing success if they put in the work and follow good practices that have been learned in the age of digital self-publishing.

Enough about me, as I'm sure you're more interested in this book's content than me. This book, as you might have guessed by the subtitle, is divided into seven easy-to-follow steps. If you follow the steps, you will become a successful self-publisher. This book will explain how to put out a good self-published product, one that can compete with the best traditionally-published book. For those who aren't the most familiar with the traditional process, Step 1 will discuss the differences between the traditional publishing model and self-publishing. Each subsequent step will explain what you need to do to get the best book written and out into the world. When you've finished all the steps, you will have what it takes to be profitable as a self-publisher. If you're looking for profitability, this isn't a one-and-done proposition. Profitable self-publishers put out multiple titles, just like profitable traditional publishers. It's a process that takes time, but it's very doable, even by those who don't fancy themselves publishers. So, sit back, relax and learn what you need to achieve your self-publishing success.

Special Note: This book was intended to be read as an ebook, so. there are a fair number of websites referenced in the book. In the original ebook, these are all clickable links the reader can click to visit instantaneously. However, that's not possible in the print version of the book. To accommodate the format change, web addresses are either listed right there in the text (when possible) or as a footnote. All web links you'll need to self-publish (such as those for service providers) are listed in the book's appendices, so don't worry about dog-earing pages so you can remember to go back and find the link. Links to informational items (such as the to the statutory damage provisions of US Copyright law), however, appear only in the text.

If you would like both the print and ebook versions of this book, print purchasers can get a discount on the ebook. The easiest way to do this is through Amazon.com's "Matchbook" service, which sells the ebook version of the print book you purchased at an extreme discount, sometimes free. If you've already purchased the print version of this book and missed out on Matchbook, drop me a line. I'll get you the ebook at a discount or free (you'll need a copy of your print book receipt). Contact me at http://rjcrayton.com/contact.

STEP 1: DETERMINE YOUR GOALS

I'm not going to send you off to make a vision board or sit with candles and meditate on what you want out of life. You can do that if you want, but that's not my style, so I'm certainly not going to suggest it for your style.

However, with self-publishing you've got to figure out what it is you want to achieve. People self-publish for all sorts of reasons. If your reason is to make money, you're going to have a different approach to self-publishing than if your reason is to put your story out there. Those approaches are going to be slightly different than the self-publisher who wants to help people (maybe you've got some killer method for life success you think everyone should know).

Sit down and think about why you're doing this. What do you hope to gain? That's going to help guide you in how you use the steps in this book. If you simply want to put out a good quality self-published product, then you'll want to focus on the first four steps. Those deal with product quality and the basics of the publishing process. If you want to promote that book (or multiple books) and have the book (or books) be profitable, you're going to want to complete all the steps, with particular emphasis on the last one.

Step 7 deals with assessment and evaluation; it's only through that evaluation process that you can figure out what works best and bring yourself to profitability. Writing success rarely comes overnight, so it's the tinkering you do in Step 7 that will help you achieve profitability. In the last section of the book, I'll provide some real-world examples of how long it has taken successful self-published authors to hit their stride.

Traditional Publishing vs. Self-Publishing

As you're mulling over your goals, let's take a minute to talk about how self-publishing compares to traditional publishing, and some of the benefits of self-publishing. If you've bought this book, you're obviously interested in self-publishing. However, you may not be well-versed in all the intricacies of the different publishing models. Let's go over them here.

Traditional Publishing.

With traditional publishing, you would normally go through a publisher (also called a publishing house). Generally publishing houses don't accept unsolicited manuscripts. To get your manuscript before a publisher, you need an agent. To get an agent, you have to write a query letter, which must tell a bit about your book and pique the agent's interest. Agents reject 95 percent of the query letters they receive. If they don't reject the query letter, agents will request either a partial or a full manuscript. Of those writers they request a manuscript from, they still reject most, taking on only a handful of new clients each year.

If you hit the jackpot and get an agent, you will generally sign a contract with the agent. Legitimate agents are paid via commission. They will not charge you a fee for any services they provide prior to them selling your book. Instead, they will take a commission, usually 15 percent of your earnings from contracts they negotiate. Legitimate agents only get paid if they sell your book. I mention legitimate because agents are not regulated and anyone can hang a shingle and call themselves an agent, including crooks. Given an agent's pay incentive, the agent will work with you to get your manuscript into tiptop shape, then try to sell it to a publisher. If the agent sells it, yay! If not, the agent, who only gets paid after selling your book, has two choices: (1) to continue to believe you're good and agree to try to sell your next project or (2) to drop you as a client. If your agent takes the second option, you are back to where you started, and you'll have to query agents for your next book (you can't re-query the same book, as most agents will not want to try to sell a manuscript that's already been rejected by several publishers).

Let's assume your book sold. At that point, in the traditional publishing process, you will sign a contract that will assign rights for your book (print and ebook, generally; possibly audio) to the publisher and spell out other publication terms. It used to be that contracts ended when a book went "out of print." Because ebooks never really go out of print, if your publisher leaves them for sale on any retail site, it's a contract that will potentially last the duration of the copyright for that book (copyright term is the life of the author + 70 years). The contract will stipulate an advance against royalties. This advance is what the publisher thinks it can, at a minimum, earn on your title. Before the publisher has to pay you any royalties from the book, your book has to earn enough to equal the amount of the advance. However, if your book does not earn the amount of the advance, you don't have to repay the publisher.

The typical advance for a first-time author is $5,000. The publisher will pay this advance in three installments: (1) one-third at the time the contract is signed, (2) one-third at the acceptance of the manuscript and (3) one-third at the time of the book's publication. From contract signing to publication, it typically takes one year to 18 months. So, it will be awhile before you get the entirety of your advance (minus your agent's commission, of course).

You may be wondering about item two, acceptance of the manu-script. The publisher is in charge of editing and cover art and publicity. The publisher will ask you to work with its editor to get the book in shape. You will not be charged to work with the editor, but you will be expected to follow the editor's advice and work with the editor on is-sues of concern. If you can't get along with the editor and are unwilling to make changes the editor suggests, your contract could fall apart on that second point, because you are not turning in a manuscript accepta-ble to the publisher. Essentially, it is the editor who determines whether the manuscript is acceptable to the publisher. Rarely do con-tracts fall apart on this issue, as the agent wants a commission and will typically try to get the author and editor to come together. However, it can happen.

With traditional publishing, the publishing house is in charge of cover art. While publishers may ask for your input, they are not obliged to take it. You could end up with a cover you hate. The publisher could even change the name of the book, and, unless your contract stipulated they couldn't, you would be stuck with it.

Publishers are in charge of distribution and marketing. They will distribute your book to some physical bookstores, but it probably won't be a lot of copies. It is also unlikely that your book will receive the best placement. The center displays when you walk into stores are called co-op, and publishers pay bookstores money to put their titles there. Publishers tend to reserve co-op money for big names like Grisham, Piccoult, or King. The publisher will also distribute your book to ebook retailers. The royalty rate paid by publishers on ebooks is 12.5 percent of list price; for print books, it ranges from 6 to 10 percent of list price, depending on whether it's a hardback or paperback. While publishers are in charge of marketing, the consensus is that most publishers don't do much publicity for newbies. With big names, they know the book should do well based on the name and are willing to put money into marketing. With newbies, publishers don't try to sink too much into what could be a failed investment. If you do well, they may do more for your next book. If you don't do well, then you just didn't do well. There are 300,000 titles published by traditional publishers each year, according to Bowker, a media company that tracks sales and issues book tracking numbers (we'll talk more about Bowker in the ISBN section). Publishers can't spend a big budget promoting 300,000 titles. They know that some books are going to fail, so they hedge their bets by promoting books they think have the best shot of succeeding with a promotional boost.

The last thing to know about traditional publishing is that you have about six months to make an impact. Unlike ebook stores, which have an almost unlimited amount of virtual shelf space, real book stores have very limited space. If your book does not sell well, the stores will take it off their shelves and return it to publishers. They'll make decisions after a month or two. After six months, the publisher will know if your title is getting too many returns or too few reorders. If that's the case, your book is done. It will still be on ebook shelves, as that costs the publisher nothing, but they'll be done with your print book. You won't be able to get your book back from the publisher to try to market and control as you want, because you'll have signed that right away in your contract.

With a failed book under your wing, it will be harder for your agent to sell future books. Your agent might still try, but it's hard because you've gone from being an unknown and unproven commodity to being a commodity with a track record of failure.

Self-Publishing.

Traditional publishing sounded a bit bleak if you didn't have instant success. Well, that's one of the main places where self-publishing has an advantage over traditional publishing. There is no bang-bam-boom timeline that says you have six months and then you're a failure. With self-publishing, your book is on the market as long as it takes to do well. But, that's one of the later advantages. Let's start at the beginning and look at some of the primary advantages when it comes to self-publishing.

Control. Self-publishers have control over the entire process and retain all their publishing rights. With the traditional process, you have control over very little — just over the book you write. You don't control whether you get picked by an agent or publisher, how much your advance is, how much marketing is done, or even which ebook stores the publisher chooses to sell your books at. However, with self-publishing, you decide (1) if your book is ready for publication and (2) when to publish it. With traditional publishing, the publisher is in charge of editing and covers and you have little say on the final decision. With self-publishing, you get to pick an editor you like and a cover you feel best expresses your book. You also get control over your rights. While we could write for hours about rights, the most important thing to note is that retaining control of all your rights is a big deal. You control rights over all categories in which your book can be produced: print, ebook, audio and film. You can sell the print rights to your work for paper books, the ebook rights for electronic books, movie rights if someone wants to make a movie based on your book, and even audio book rights. Rights tend to be assigned based on the region they're to be sold in, so you can sell print rights in the United States, or print rights in Spain, and retain all other rights. In the traditional model, publishers tend to want all print and ebook rights for the entire world. With self-publishing, there's no struggle with the publisher. Or you could say, as a self-publisher, you assign your rights to the publisher; only you're the publisher, so any battles over rights always go your way. In the self-publishing process, you and your heirs get to benefit from your work for the entire term of the copyright. (For more on heirs, see the *Appendix D* article, *When your Books Outlive You*, p. 190.)

Responsibility. While you have control over all those aspects, with self-publishing, you are responsible for doing all the things the publisher normally does. You have to find cover artists, editors, write blurbs, select marketing material, format your book for electronic and print, and distribute it to the retailers where you want it sold. If you don't want to be responsible for these things, then self-publishing is not for you. However, if this represents a challenge you want, then self-publishing is great.

We're at the end of Step 1. I hope you have your goal in mind. Write it down, as you'll need to refer back to it later. In the remaining steps, we'll discuss all the things you need to do to put out a great self-published product. At the end of each step, I'm inserting a checklist as a quick way to review the key points of the chapter.

Step 1 Checklist

_____ Determine your goal (what you want from self-publishing)

_____ Write down your goal

STEP 2: WRITE GOOD BOOKS

You've completed Step 1 and figured out your goal. This was really important, because it's going to direct everything you do from here on out. The next step of the process is, oddly enough, even more important than that first step. In fact, it is the most important part of your process. You need to write good books. Bad books don't sell. Now, don't get snarky with me and tell me about that bestseller that you think is total crap in terms of writing. The readers who bought it would disagree with you, as would the author. But, we're digressing. The essential thing to know — whether you are writing for profit or for other reasons — is that what says the most about your book is the product itself. It has to be good. It has to meet the needs of its buyers so they feel it is a quality product.

There are a few things that people think of when it comes to book quality: a compelling and coherent tale that is free of grammar and spelling errors. In this step, you will learn some strategies to help you produce a good book. Those include writing a lot, developing a writing habit, writing in genres that work for you, being accountable for your work, and getting beta readers. I also include notes on pseudonyms and when to release your books.

Write a Lot

You need to write a lot. Yes, I said that. Even if you feel you have a single magnum opus, the writing process improves dramatically the more you write.

I would recommend writing complete pieces, and, at a minimum, tens of thousands of words worth of them. If you truly think you have only one magnum opus and don't want to write multiple books, then write short stories — or essays, if nonfiction is your thing. Whatever you write should be a complete piece, which is one that has a beginning, middle, and end. Writing never-ending stories or little bits of unfinished ideas don't get you used to the process of finishing. So, write complete pieces. This will serve as great practice for people who want to write several books, as well as people who believe they only have one book to write.

If you plan to make money self-publishing or know you'd like to publish several books over the course of your lifetime, then I suggest writing multiple books. You can include some short stories or essays, too, but writing books will help improve your craft and understanding of the process. More specifically, writing a lot will help you figure out what works best for your process. For the people who want to self-publish for profit, writing several books will help them build their arsenal of books.

While there are people who write one book and decide to publish it, those people often find it works out better to write two full books before publishing one. You'll be amazed at the personal growth you get as a writer, and how much better the final product looks. While I think you should write at least two full books before publishing, I don't say you can't publish that first one. You have to be the judge of your quality and experience. Whether you publish the first book or not, after you've written that second book, go back over the first one and see how it looks to you. See what things you can improve to make it better. Your goal is to have a good book.

Writing Habit

Every writer should develop a daily writing habit. This will help you achieve whatever goal you've chosen, whether it be to complete one self-published work or to write a slew of self-published books.

I recommend writing as the first thing you do when you sit down with free time. Don't respond to emails. Don't read your favorite blogs. Don't check out the Facebook writing group or your Twitter feed. Sit down and write first. Writing is going to be the thing that improves your chances of success, so that is the thing you should do first.

For writers who are interested in simply putting out the best story they can, writing to your comfort level will help you. If you want to set a time limit and whatever you get done in that time is good, then go for it. If you think a word count target is good, then pick one and do that. It's going to be about what you feel comfortable with. The more you write, the better at it you will become.

If your goal is monetary success, then you've got to have output, and you need to have a daily word count goal. I would recommend a minimum word count goal of 1,000 words per day, five days a week. That translates to a rough output of 260,000 words annually, or four 65,000-word books per year. Again, that's just my recommendation. If you're working two jobs already and it's not doable, then you can't do it. However, for those who want to make money, the thing that is going to get you there is having more books, just like traditional publishers. The only way for self-published authors to add more books to their arsenal is to write them. (If you're publishing someone else's books, you're not a self-publisher; you're a small publisher.)

Writing 1,000 words a day will get you the kind of volume you'll need to eventually get monetary success. There's a great article[1] by Dean Wesley Smith discussing how much the famous "pulp fiction" authors wrote in a typical year. It wasn't uncommon for a pulp writer to produce 2 million words annually. That's averaging almost 5,500 words per day every day. That's a lot of writing. What I've suggested is less than one-fifth of that amount, and I'm only asking you to commit to that number five days a week, rather than seven. I think that recommendation is very doable for writers who want self-publishing to be their primary business.

Writers should also read, too. Try to read within the genre you're writing. When you read other people's novels, read with a mind to steal. No, I'm not suggesting plagiarism. Don't steal actual words, but you do want to steal technique. If a writer does something that you really like in a book, try to figure out what worked about it. Is that a technique you can use in your own book? Also, look at what doesn't work. If something in a book makes you cringe, you should file that away as an unsuccessful technique.

The last thing I'll say in this section is to also make a backing-up habit. Be sure to have a system of backing up your manuscripts daily. The last thing you want is to finish your manuscript and then have your

---

[1] The New World of Writing: Pulp Speed, http://www.deanwesleysmith.com/the-new-world-of-writing-pulp-speed/

hard drive crash, your manuscript disappearing with it. Some people use backup services that continuously backup their data while they write. Other people back up to Google Drive or DropBox at the end of the day. Still, others use a flash drive to back up their work at the end of the day. Any method is fine, so long as you don't lose your work.

What to Write?

This section is mainly aimed at those who are interested in self-publishing as a way to make money. If you want to self-publish just to get your book into the world, or for some other reason that isn't earnings-based, then write what you want. For those who've decided they'd ultimately like to be earning a decent amount of money through self-publishing, this section offers some mild guidance on profitable genres and book styles (specifically, series).

People who want to make money often ask, "Which genres earn the most money?" First, and most importantly, you should write what you enjoy and are good at writing. Bad books that you don't enjoy writing won't sell, no matter how popular the genre or book style. Them's the breaks, folks. Figure out the genres you like writing or think you could like writing. Once you've done that, you can see if those mesh with the most popular genres.

The genres that are most popular, in terms of sales[2], are romance, mystery and thriller and science fiction/fantasy. Within romance, people have found that erotica does well (especially in the wake of *50 Shades of Grey*). However, if you don't like writing about sex, your erotica isn't going to be very good. So, pick something you like and write that. If you love chick lit and you love mysteries, and you want to earn money, then definitely write a couple of mysteries, because as a genre, mystery sells better than horror. But, you can still write your horror tome, too, because your success is going to be based on producing high-quality volume. Each time you publish a book, it's a chance for a fan to find you. Once a fan finds you and likes your stuff, they're more likely to purchase other stuff you've written. So, the person who wants to make money on this endeavor has to get multiple publications out there. We're going to talk more about multiple titles when we get to marketing strategies.

---

[2] Scroll down to Number of Titles in e-Book Genre Bestseller Lists, http://authorearnings.com/report/the-report/

As a quick note here when discussing multiple titles, series of books tend to sell well. So, if you want to write a series, that's a good idea from a strategy standpoint. There are two kinds of series: (1) ones that simply use the same character and similar narrative, such as the Nancy Drew mysteries, the James Bond books, or Sue Grafton's Alphabet mysteries, and (2) ones that tell a linear narrative over several books, such as the *Harry Potter, The Hunger Games,* or the *Divergent* series. The second group is sometimes referred to as "serial" novels rather than just a series. However, be forewarned that when you write serial novels, if the first book doesn't sell, it's often hard to market the related books because they're dependent on readers purchasing book one. Series that start with a completely new story each time, but just keep the same characters, make it easier to market books that are later in the series, as the reader doesn't feel the need to read other books in the series in order to enjoy the present one. I'll talk more about series and serial novels when we get to the section on free (p. 100).

Accountability for Your Work

I was debating where to put this in the book, because I didn't want to be discouraging. However, talking about it after you've written a book runs the risk of you having to go back and make serious changes. Since I prefer avoiding problems up front, rather than dealing with them later, we'll discuss this issue now. Here's the deal: you are accountable for your book. In the United States, where I live, we have a Constitutional right to Freedom of Speech. That means the government generally can't censor or put citizens in jail for something we say. *The right to freedom of speech protects citizens from government persecution for their words; it does not protect citizens from being fired by their employers for something they say or from being sued for something they say.*

If you are a teacher and go to school every day and notice how lax the security is, it might occur to you to write a novel about a teacher who shoots all his students. While this is perfectly acceptable legally, this may have certain repercussions for you at work. It could even violate some of your teachers' conduct code, depending on how broad it is for your school district. A teacher also might want to consider whether he or she wants to write erotica while at their current job. It's not to say you'll never publish these things, but if you depend on a day job to support your writing, consider how your writing might impact that day job.

In late 2014, a fire chief in Atlanta was fired [3]after he published what the media described as a "homophobic book." The book included only about a paragraph on homosexuals, but it was enough that his boss fired him. At the time this book went to press, the fire chief had sued to get his job back, contending that the firing violated his religious freedom (not free speech, you'll note). The case was not decided at press time, but I think the ultimate point I'm making is that things you say can have consequences. Authors can write whatever they want, but I think it's important for them to evaluate what the consequences might be so they can be prepared. Some people may choose to write things that might get them fired, feeling they believe strongly enough in it to deal with the consequences, while others think to themselves, "I really need my paycheck," and choose to delay that book or omit the problematic areas.

Now, let's say you don't depend on a paycheck. You're independently wealthy; a trust fund babe who relies on dividends rather than an employer or dealings with the public to make your cash. You'll want to think about lawsuits. We talked earlier about people who want to publish because they think they can help someone with their ideas. In those instances, you need to check if your advice can harm people. This is noticeable in books on dieting or other health tomes. If you lost 50 pounds by drinking a shot glass of lighter fluid each day, and you're mentioning it as medical advice or writing a book called *The Lighter Fluid Diet*, you open yourself up to lawsuit and claims associated with medical products. If you have anything that's advice laden that might cause injury to your readers, it's a good idea to have an attorney look the book over to see if you're opening yourself up to liability. Also, if you are a memoir writer, you need to get a signed release from people you will be writing about in your book, or you can be subject to lawsuit. But, you say, "Wait! I read celebrity memoirs all the time and there's no way everyone in that book signed a release." True. But, celebrities are not entitled the same right to privacy as those not in the public eye. If you're a relative unknown, as are the people in your books, they have the non-celebrity right to privacy, and you might violate it by publishing a book that discloses their personal life (even in the context of how

---

[3] Atlanta Fire Chief Fired over Homophobic Book, http://www.mhp-books.com/the-fire-chief-who-wrote-the-homophobic-book-has-been-fired/

they interacted with you) without their permission or consent. Generally items of public record can be published (your parents got divorced), but items only the parties involved know (your parents divorced because your father slept with your mother's best friend) can violate privacy. For memoirs, get consent and consult an attorney if you are unsure which things require consent. In the context of nonfiction, you obviously can't write things that are untrue about others, or you expose yourself to a libel lawsuit.

I think I've hit the basic areas of concern here, but do check out the *Appendix D* article, *Legal Issues for Authors* (p. 187), if you'd like some more info.

Pseudonyms

Since we're talking about accountability, let's look at pseudonyms. Using a pseudonym is one way to distance your true name from a work. People use pseudonyms for all sorts of reasons. One of the most famous writers of his time, Samuel Clemens, is known primarily by his pseudonym, Mark Twain.

In addition to providing a layer of distance between your real name and your writing name, pseudonyms are a way to brand. Some authors write in multiple genres and use pseudonyms to help the reader quickly assess what type of book they're getting. For example, an author might write romances under one name, while writing mysteries under another. The author often doesn't care that the public knows they have a pseudonym; the pseudonym is there specifically so the customer knows what type of book they're getting. A romance writer might use a pseudonym to separate "sweet" (i.e. no sex) titles from erotic titles. I have a friend who writes both young adult and erotica, and, for obvious reasons, he uses a pseudonym because he doesn't want his YA readers to pick up an erotic title because they like his work and want to read everything by him.

I mentioned before that you are accountable for your work. Using a pseudonym doesn't make you any less accountable. It just means that people are not immediately going to associate you with the work, and that may be all you need for the purposes of a job. Many writers of erotica write under pseudonyms. Often times they use a pseudonym to sound sexier on the cover, with an author name like Pussycat Dawl or Trixie Leggz. Erotica writers also use pseudonyms if they don't want the casual friend, observer, or employer to Google them and find their name associated with erotic titles.

If you just want an extra layer between your identity and your real self, a pseudonym is fine. However, a pseudonym does not guarantee no one will learn your identity. Most times, when you register a copyright for a work, your real name is linked to that pseudonym in that public record. (You can register a copyright under your pseudonym, but you have to have some document, such as a "Doing Business As" license in your state, that legally — and usually, publicly — connects you to the pseudonym.) Also, if you have an ex-spouse or ex-partner who wants to tell people your identity, then that is their prerogative (unless you made them sign a nondisclosure agreement). Obviously, if someone chooses to sue you, the ebook company you are selling through (such as Amazon) will provide your actual legal name to the court, per any legal filing requests. A pseudonym is great if you just don't want the casual observer to know who you are, but it's not a foolproof way to hide your identity.

A Note about Author Names

When creating a pseudonym or deciding what part of your real name you want to write under (Martha Williams, M.T. Williams, etc.), do check to see if the name is already in use. While you generally can use your own name for your work, you might be prohibited from using a name already in use that is not your own. For example, I know of an author named Stephen King (his website is http://theotherstephen king.com), and he uses Stephen H. King to write with because that is his legal name. However, you can't pick James Patterson for your pseudonym (or, you can, but you'll probably get a call from Mr. Patterson's attorneys telling you to quit that). While the Patterson example was given to elicit a chuckle, even if you don't use a currently famous author's name, you might not want confusion with unknown authors either. If you write young adult and your pseudonym is Missy Barker, you don't want to be confused with the Missy Barker who has published 56 erotic novels. The same holds true for your real name. You might want to use a pseudonym if another writer who has the same name as you is already using the name. However, with your real name, you can generally use it regardless of who else is using it. You have to determine whether you want to be different or don't mind confusion. What's the harm in confusion? Well, if the other Stephen King is more famous than you, when people search for your name at online vendors, guess which author will appear first in the search results? It's unlikely readers will find you unless they click through several screens of the more famous author.

Beta Readers Improve Your Book

Now that we've gone over some things that will help you get your book written, and you've determined whether there are any problematic issues, it's time to get your book ready to publish. The first thing you want to do is make the best book possible. That means don't write your first draft and then publish it. Read it again, and see what you think. Then read it again and make changes. Try to get your book up to the level that you think is actually publishable. That means correcting for grammar and punctuation to the best of your ability. Read through it thoroughly and run your computer's spellcheck.

After you've made your book to the best you think it can be, it's time to get feedback on it. "From whom?" you ask. From beta readers. Those are people who are willing to read your book and tell you honestly what they think. They don't just say things like, "I liked it" or "I didn't like it." Beta readers should give concrete feedback.

Where do you find these cool beta reader people? Ideally, they'll come from people you know. You write, so you probably enjoy reading and maybe some of your friends do, too. Those are people you can ask to beta read. If you're in a writers group, you might ask some of your writer friends to beta read (remember, reciprocity is expected within reason; if someone beta reads for you, you should also beta for them, if they request it). And if you don't have these people in your lives, you can always look online. There are several online groups where you can ask for beta readers. These are going to be people you've never met, so you're going to want to participate in the groups for a little bit and see which people you think would do a good job offering feedback. Here are a couple of online sites where you can find beta readers:

- Goodreads Beta Reader Group, https://www. gooreads.com/group/show/50920-beta-reader-group
- World Literary Group Beta & Critique Group, http://www.worldliterarycafe.com/forum/125
- Absolute Write Beta Readers, http://absolute write.com/forums/forumdisplay.php?s=0cd99b5072c45 e00673dd608ae56bde1&f=30

Once you've found people who agree to be beta readers, send the manuscript with questions you want them to think about as they read the book. Here's a sample list of questions you can offer your beta readers for a fiction book.

1. What parts bored you?
2. Which parts were page turners you couldn't put down?
3. Was anything confusing?
4. Which characters did you like best (and why)?
5. Which characters did you dislike (and why)?
6. Were there any characters you found so annoying you wished they weren't in the book?

For a nonfiction book, you can ask questions 1-3 in the fiction list along with these three questions.

1. Was there information in the book that you felt was useless or irrelevant?
2. Was there a place where you wanted more information but didn't get it?
3. Did you feel you got what you were promised from this book? (This question is important for self-help guides, or autobiographies with a message, and can be honed more depending on the premise of the book.)

If beta readers pick up the book with questions in mind, they'll know what things to flag mentally, and put down on a list for you. Beta readers are people, and people are all different. If a beta reader gives you feedback you disagree with, you don't have to do anything with it. You can chalk up certain feedback as someone who just didn't like the book. Not everyone is going to like every book (check out the 1-star reviews for JK Rowling's mega successful *Harry Potter* books). However, don't just ignore unpleasant feedback. If you initially don't agree with the feedback, set it aside and wait for a couple more beta readers to get back to you. Once you have a few beta reader thoughts, you can make some decisions about the types of changes you'll make.

Generally, you make changes based on the fact that you feel the beta readers have hit the mark. Often times, it's something you were worried about yourself, and other times, it's something you hadn't thought of, but it makes total sense once the beta reader points it out. If you get beta reader feedback you disagree with, you should strongly consider making a change if several beta readers say the same thing. If you've had four people look at the manuscript and they all remark on the same problem, then that item needs to be examined more closely. Now, it's your book and you're responsible for it (sorry, I hope I'm not beating a dead horse with that comment). You have to live with what's in it. If you truly don't want to change things based on the feedback, you don't have to. But, when several people are telling you the same thing, it's a sign that a fix needs to be made. Perhaps you keep the feel of the item that's giving your beta readers problems, but you reword it in a way that addresses their concerns.

Famous, well-heeled authors use beta readers too. Audrey Niffenegger, famous for the *The Time Traveler's Wife*, made huge structural changes to that book based on beta reader feedback. In this interview[4], she says, "Originally it was thematically organized, but early readers found that confusing. Several people suggested following Clare's chronology, which is mostly what I ended up doing."

It's important not to be defensive with beta reader feedback. Look at it and accept it for what it is: the opinion of a person who was KIND ENOUGH to read your book. Another thing to remember with beta readers is that your feedback is only as good as the beta reader. If the person is a close relative, and they're not going to give you any critical feedback and just cheer on the good parts, you need to recognize that and take it for what it's worth. There are some beta readers who are incredibly critical, dissatisfied, and blunt in their assessments, and you have to take that for what it's worth, too. The best beta readers add thoughtful, insightful comments, and if you find them, they're golden. Keep them. Love them. Cherish them. Buy them a gift card at their favorite coffee shop or bakery for Christmas or their birthday, as they're worth gold and you want their feedback.

When you give your work to beta readers, in addition to giving them those questions, you also want to give them a time frame for returning your work. One month is standard for a complete novel. However, three weeks is not considered unduly harsh. If it's a shorter work, like a novella or short story, then you can ask for a quicker turnaround time. As a rule of thumb, I'd suggest one week per 25,000 words of

---

[4] Audrey Niffenegger interview, https://exileonninthstreet.word-press.com/2008/11/19/time-bending-an-interview-with-audrey-niffenegger/

text. Though, if you have a fantasy novel or something that runs longer, seeking one month for the whole thing is fine because a month is the standard.

I'll reiterate here that you need to offer the best book you can to beta readers. If your book is riddled with typos and seems haphazard, your beta readers are going to feel like they don't have to put much into it. I don't believe you need to get your book edited prior to sending it to beta readers; but do try to send them the same book you'd send to an editor (who will charge you more if your book is riddled with errors; we'll talk more about that in Editing, p. 25). If you present beta readers with a quality product, they're more likely to present you with quality feedback. If you don't hear back from some of your beta readers in the time period you specified, you can send them a gentle email reminding them that you look forward to their feedback. However, recognize that some people will flake out and not finish it. It happens. Move on. You don't have to use them again.

After beta readers give you feedback, **ALWAYS *thank them***. Here's some boiler plate language you can use.

DEAR _____,

Thank you so much for taking the time to read my book (Give book name). I appreciate all of your thoughtful comments. While I may not use every suggestion you made, rest assured that I looked at them all and considered what you said. Thanks again.

YOUR NAME

It's simple and appreciative.

After you've received beta reader feedback, and figured out which criticism is valid, take one more pass at your book, making any corrections necessary based on the feedback. After that, you'll want to get your book edited.

Timing the Release of Your Books

This is a quick note directed at those whose goal is to make money self-publishing. Like I said before, you'll want to write more than one book. Traditional publishers don't stay in business by publishing one writer or one book. In the world of traditional publishing, a lot of books don't make money. Publishers earn money by having multiple titles, which strengthens the chance of one of the titles becoming a breakout success and earning money. To make money as a self-publisher, you're going to want to have several titles out. Fans will read one, and if they like it, will move on to the next; but they need titles to move on to.

In terms of that, some people choose to write several books before they publish any, so that they can put out titles at a regular interval that is speedier than their normal pace would allow. This quicker release schedule allows momentum to build. For example, if a person wants to put out a title every four months in the first year, but it takes that person six months to write a book, then he or she might write three books entirely before starting the publishing process. That way, the author can publish at four month intervals initially. Some of the more successful self-published authors, like HM Ward, publish a book every other month.

If you plan to write several books and then time release them at a quicker pace, at some point you're going to fall behind. However, people who choose this strategy are OK with that, feeling the early momentum is more important than sustaining the quicker pace.

Some people prefer to publish as they complete a work, and not worry about the lag between books. You have to decide which method will work best for you. If you want to write several books before publishing them at set intervals, then write the first book and, while that book is out with beta readers, start writing the second book. When book one comes back from the beta readers, you can feel free to move on to the next steps in the process for book one, or continue writing the book you were working on. If you prefer to complete one book fully before moving on to another, then you can go through all the steps in this process that take you right up to the point before you hit publish. Only, you won't hit publish until your timetable calls for that book to get released and you have others waiting in the wings.

In terms of timing, enjoy those weeks while your book is out with beta readers. That's a great time to work on the next book in the project. It's often hard to split focus when making edits based on beta feedback, so using the time when the document is being read by others is a great idea.

If you're planning to write a series (either the serial or a stand-alone with same characters), be sure to check out the *Appendix D* article, *Tips on Creating a Story Bible* (p. 161). If you're unfamiliar with a story bible, it is a document that helps you keep track of characters when you're writing a series. It will help you maintain consistency in your tale, especially if it is quite involved.

So, this is the end of Step 2. If you've finished this step, your book is in pretty good shape. You've gotten into a writing habit that works for you, gotten your book written, feel good with your accountability for what's been written, and have gotten some beta reader feedback that's improved your manuscript. At this point in the process, you've really done all the stuff a writer who wants to be published needs to do. If you had an abrupt change of heart and decided you wanted to go the traditional publishing route, you'd have a great manuscript to shop to agents, and possibly be working on your next book (depending on your goals). The next step is where we get into the parts that really set the self-published author apart from the traditional author. Step 3 is where we polish your book to professional. That step is where you start doing all the things necessary to release a book to the marketplace: editing, cover art, and a book blurb. So, if you're ready, let's head on to Step 3.

Step 2 Checklist

Writing Good Books

_____ Set writing habit goal

_____ Determined what you plan to write about

_____ Evaluated work ideas/actual work for accountability issues

_____ Decided if you will use a pseudonym

_____ Checked to see whether author name is already in use

Beta Readers

_____ Identified beta readers willing to read

_____ Cleaned up manuscript to best of your ability (thorough read-through and spell-check)

_____ Sent manuscript to beta readers with questions

_____ Received beta feedback

_____ Nudged beta readers who did not respond

_____ Thanked beta readers

_____ Incorporated changes based on beta reader feedback

Time releasing

_____ Determined if this strategy is for you, and if so, created a schedule that works for you

STEP 3: POLISHING TO PROFESSIONAL

Writing a good book (Step 2) is critical to the process, but failing to polish the book will undermine all the good work you did in Step 2.

In this step, you begin doing the things that make an author a self-publisher. The first two steps in this book are something that all writers — whether traditional or self-published — can do. While self-published writers are going to have different goals than ones who want to traditionally publish, traditional writers could still benefit from these steps. However, now is where the rubber meets the road. So far we've been planning our journey — figuring out the destination, checking the GPS directions. Now we're ready to drive. Whereas a traditional author would be waiting for a cab to drive by, the self-published author is in the seat, ignition turned, and putting a foot on the pedal.

To polish your book to the level of a professional publisher, you need to get it edited, get a great cover, and write an awesome book description. We'll go over each of these parts in the following pages.

Editing

Your book should include proper grammar and punctuation, otherwise it will look unprofessional and readers will leave bad reviews. Some may not even finish the book if it's poorly edited. You don't want that, so one of the most important things you're going to do as a self-publisher is get your book edited.

How do you go about this? There are a couple of options. One is to hire an editor. Hiring an editor has the advantage of it being professional and likely accurate; however, it can be expensive. The other option is to get a friend to edit it for free. If you go that route, you have to trust that the friend has a good knowledge of English grammar and is excellent at catching mistakes.

So, let's look briefly at both options. I'm going to start with paying for an editor, and I'll say upfront that I do recommend hiring an editor.

If you hire a professional editor, you have several editing choices. You can get a substantive edit, which looks at the overall plot and structure; a copy edit, which looks at grammar, punctuation, and style; and a proofread, which is a final look for very basic grammar or punctuation errors. You can hire all three types of editors. I'll explain a bit more about each one and why people sometimes use all three.

A "substantive edit," sometimes called a "structural edit," looks over the plot and structure of your novel with the goal of fine-tuning the overall product. Grammar and punctuation will not be the primary focus of this edit. This edit is designed to tighten up the book so it reads well, and may involve moving scenes around, deleting plot lines, or otherwise rewriting the book so it flows better. This type of edit is called a "developmental edit" when you hire the editor to work with you as you start writing the story, so the editor can help and guide you through the process. Whatever you call it — substantive, structural, or developmental — this type of edit can be very expensive, so most self-publishers skip it and use beta readers for this type of feedback.

Many self-publishers skip this step, but one beta reader (see, I use them) pointed out that it sounded like I am anti-editing. This is not true. I think every book should be edited. The question really is, "How?" If you have the money for a substantive edit and feel it would be useful, go for it. Please note, I said, "If you have the money." A substantive edit can cost several thousand dollars. For this money, the editor is going to work with you and give you concrete suggestions on how to fix problems they see in your work. Beta readers, while helpful in finding problems, often don't suggest fixes or don't suggest fixes that work within the context of your novel or writing style. An editor you're paying should be more helpful than a beta reader, offering targeted suggestions and fixes based on your novel and writing style.

Many authors like that type of editing for its solution-based approach and collaborative spirit. If you're one of them and have the money to spend, then go for it. A word of caution with any editor, but in particular a substantive editor: do some research and find a good editor who is willing to give you references. Talk to the references to find out about the editor's working style so you can get a good fit. The last thing you want is to spend hundreds or thousands of dollars on an edit and learn the editor is an overbearing Mr. Bossypants who wants to change your voice to his own. With a substantive edit in particular, you need an editor who can express tips and suggestions to improve your story without stamping out your style or voice. And while many self-publishers skip the structural edit, a lot don't. Indies Unlimited conducted a survey of self-publishers' processes [5]and found that 44 percent of respondents used a content editor (another term for a structural edit).

The next type of edit to discuss is the copy edit. This editor will look for grammar, punctuation, sentence flow, clarity, and overall style and consistency. Style and consistency cannot be overlooked. If you call your main character "Prince Hubert" in most instances and you call him "prince Hubert" somewhere, your copy editor will catch that style inconsistency. In that example, it's also a grammar error. A good copy editor will help keep everything consistent. Also, this edit should make sure everything reads in a way that makes sense, and is grammatically correct. This editor will fix the occasional sentence that is worded in a way that is awkward or confusing. However, if every sentence is awkward and confusing, they may choose not to edit your work. Copy editors have varying rates. Some can be expensive (thousands of dollars), while others can be cheaper (a couple of hundred dollars). Some editors post rates on their website, while others tell you they need to see a sample of your work before they give you a quote. If every sentence is a mangled mess, the copy editor may quote high or tell you to see a structural editor first, and come back afterward. If the work is pretty clean, they will likely quote you a lower price because there is less work for them to do.

The final type of edit you can get is a proofread. Here, the editor is just looking at whether or not there are grammatical or punctuation errors. If the sentence is mangled and confusing, but grammatically correct, the proofer does not care. The proofread is just to make sure there are no obvious, glaring errors. You can hire all three editors, if

---

[5] Self-Publisher Process survey results part 2, http://www.indiesunlimited.com/2015/03/27/and-the-publishing-process-survey-says-part-2/

you wish, and you will hire them in the exact order I described: a structural edit, followed by a copy edit, followed by a proofread. That would be the way to go in an ideal world.

However, self-publishers — especially those starting out — tend to have limited budgets that require watching every penny. If that is the situation you are in, I would recommend hiring only a copy editor. I think you get the most bang for your buck with a copy editor. This editor will catch the grammatical errors and will help you with your most egregious sentences, and should return to you a manuscript that is pretty much error free. Now, no one is perfect, so a proofreader can be hired after a copy edit. However, a good copy editor should give you a book that's publishable. With a good copy edit, you should be able to do the final proof yourself, if you're decent with grammar and editing.

I've mentioned a few times that editing can cost thousands of dollars. So, how much does a good editor cost you? It depends. You can find some editors who will edit the entire manuscript for as little as $150, but most cost more, between $400 and $3,000. If you hire an editor, be sure to check the person's references and talk to previous clients about how easy they are to work with and whether they meet deadlines. Editors are often booked a few months in advance and may take a month to edit your manuscript. You need to build that time into your publication schedule.

How does one find a paid editor? Well, the best thing to do is ask other authors you know. After that, there's a group called the Editor's guild (http://www.edsguild.org/), and it lists members who edit, with links to their websites. A site called http://www.peopleperhour.com offers some editors at lower prices. This site is not specifically geared toward editing and offers all sorts of service, so be sure to check reviews and references when hiring an editor here.

In terms of editor pricing, one thing you'll find is editors often don't put their prices on their websites. This can be frustrating, as writers are well aware of their budgets, and it wastes time to inquire about an edit that you would never even consider because it's going to cost $3,000. On a personal and practical level, I prefer editors who at least give a price range (such as $400 to $600 or $.05 to $.08 per word) on their website, as opposed to editors who say, "Contact me" for pricing info. The reason some editors don't list their prices is they don't want to commit to the standard price for a project that takes more time and effort to complete than the norm (one with a lot of grammatical errors). That's why they want you to contact them. Generally, they offer to do a sample edit, where they edit up to five pages of the work you want edited. This gives you both an opportunity to see the other's work. Before turning over your document to an editor, you should get it in the best shape possible, as it can help keep your editing costs as low as possible.

If you've just read this info about pricing and have said to yourself that you can't afford any of it, then don't panic. Many self-published authors can't afford an editor, especially if it is a small project they're not sure will make money or one they're doing for personal fulfillment. In these instances, I would recommend finding a grammar-savvy friend or loved one to serve as your editor. If you're a grammar-savvy writer and know other grammar-savvy writers, you can often trade manuscripts for an edit. However, in any situation where you're asking someone not trained as an editor to do this, you need to be sure they can handle it. If it's a fellow writer, you should each swap a chapter to see if you're both happy with the mistakes the other person catches. If it's a friend or loved one, you've probably seen documents they've proofread or edited. If you haven't, give them a fake document (say, "Hey, I have to write this letter to my senator; can you look it over for errors?") to see what kind of feedback they provide.

Accepting Your Edits

If you hire an editor, they will probably work with your manuscript in Microsoft Word, using the track changes feature. Often they will send you two copies of the document: one that has all the changes accepted so it reads like a final document, and one that has the changes prior to acceptance. If you use the tracked document, you have to go in and accept all the changes the editor made piecemeal.

If you don't like seeing all the minor changes the editor makes, just read through the changed document to see if it all jibes for you. However, if you want to get a sense of what the editor did, go in and look at the track changes and accept each one.

If you didn't hire an editor, but instead got a friend to do it, you still need to go back and look over the edits they did. If the friend used track changes, go back and look over the document the way you would with a professional editor. If your friend marked up a hard copy for you, and you've got to input the edits, then you're going to want to take your time with it and make sure you get every change made correctly.

Whether you go with an editor or a friend, once editing changes are made, let the document sit untouched a couple of days; then go back and read through it one last time. It's very difficult to catch all errors, so that final read-through will give you a shot at catching any stray problems. Be careful to mainly fix errors and not recraft sentences, or else you could introduce new errors. Even if you've hired a copy editor and a proofreader, you may still want to look at it one last time.

Covers

Maybe people shouldn't judge a book by its cover, but they do. If people are going to judge your book by its cover anyway, then you might as well try to get a perfect 10. The cover is going to be a crucial element to your novel. You want a cover that both captures the spirit of your novel and the genre your novel occupies.

First up, let's take a quick second to discuss genre, which is the category that describes your books. These are some broad genres: romance, science fiction, thrillers, and mysteries. Within each genre, you can drill down further to subgenres. Within science fiction, there's dystopia, post-apocalyptic, space travel, and time travel. Within romance, there's erotica, historical romance, and paranormal. So, if your novel's genre is historical romance, its cover should look and feel similar to other historical romance novels.

How do you know what covers in your genre look like? Simple. Go to http://amazon.com, click on Departments, scroll down to Books>Kindle Store. Once there, across the top of the page, you'll see several links. Click the one for Best Sellers. That will list all the Kindle best sellers. On the left, under Best Sellers, you will see a bunch of genres. Click there to find the best sellers in your genre. You want your covers to look similar to those. (If you're still unclear how to find it, see this quick tutorial: http://rjcrayton.com/sp/tutorials.)

With cover design, the types of things you are looking for are placement of text, the type of picture used, and the type of fonts used. When looking at covers, you might notice romance novels have a picture of a man and a woman and curly fonts, while sci-fi novels have something ominous, like a rising moon or a distant star, along with a wide san serif font. San serif fonts are the kinds that don't have a little edge sticking out to decorate them, and include Arial and Helvetica.

Serif fonts would include Times New Roman and Georgia. For more on fonts, check out this article by the Book Designer, http://www.the bookdesigner.com/2011/08/5-great-fonts-for-book-covers.

Now that you know what you want, you just have to figure out how to get it. There are three ways to get a cover for your book: create your own, purchase a premade cover, or have an artist design your cover.

The "create your own" option is one a lot of self-publishers go with because they don't want to spend money on a cover designer. This option can work well if you're familiar with graphic design. However, it can go horribly awry and look terrible if you really have no idea what you're doing. If you have a cover concept, create it using the software you have, and see how it looks. If it looks awful in terms of execution, but you love the concept, then you can try to figure out how you can make it look better yourself, or you can use that as an example when you hire a designer — telling the designer you'd like something similar, but that actually looks professional.

If you're going to create your own cover (or at least give it a try), here are a couple of tips. First, get good stock photography. Stock photos are ones that are licensed for use on covers. You can't just grab photos off the internet, because photos are copyrighted and can't be used just because you find them online. You need licensed photographs (read the license, as it may have some prohibitions, but most licenses allow for print and ebook covers). You can get stock photos from several fee-based sites like http://www.shutterstock.com, www.depositphotos.com, or www.periodimages.com (great for romance covers). Wiki Commons (http://commons.wikimedia.org/wiki/Main_Page) offers free images, which are generally licensed for any use at no cost. Another great site that offers licensed images for free is www.pixabay.com. Anytime a photograph includes an identifiable person, you need not only the photographer's consent to use the image, but also the consent of the subject. Sites where you pay money for photographs have signed model release forms (the consent I just mentioned). That's part of what you pay for when you use those sites. However, on Wiki Commons, and Pixabay, there might not be the signed model release, so be cautious when it comes to using free stock photography that includes an identifiable face. If the photo includes a couple holding hands and you can only see the back of their heads, you shouldn't need a model release because the faces are not identifiable. A couple looking longingly at each other where both faces are clearly visible would require a model release.

The second tip for making a cover yourself is to go big with the title. Most self-publishers are going to make their money on ebooks, and ebooks are sold via thumbnail shots of the cover. Your title has to be legible in thumbnail and the cover has to look good in thumbnail. Nothing that is integral to your cover — whether it be the title or image — should be tiny or hard to read in the thumbnail image. KS Brooks, one of the many awesome author gurus at Indies Unlimited, wrote this fabulous blog post (http://www.indiesunlimited.com/2014/07/25/title-envy) on title size (because yes, baby, size matters, and anyone who tells you otherwise is a liar).

You can use any image editing software with drawing capabilities to create covers. Adobe Photoshop is the Cadillac piece of software, but like a Cadillac, it's pricey (now it's only available via yearly subscription plans). A writer I know does his covers in Microsoft Paint, which comes free on most Windows computers. A great piece of free software that is similar in scope to Photoshop is Gimp (http://www.gimp.com). I've downloaded Gimp and find it allows you to do a great deal when it comes to cover creation. However, Gimp is not at all intuitive and has a steep learning curve. When I first started using the software, I'd spend hours doing something as simple as changing a person's hair color in the picture. This is because I had to look up online tutorials and experiment with it. If you plan on making most of your covers, I think it's worth the time to learn Gimp.

In the "create your own" option, some people opt to go with Amazon or Create Space's "cover creator" tools. These tools are online software housed on servers (at Amazon or CreateSpace) that allow you create a professional-looking, standard book cover. The cover creators offer you a few choices of stock photography as well as themes you can use for your book. I tried the cover creator at CreateSpace and was unimpressed. I didn't feel like it gave enough options, and I found it difficult to use. Additionally, book covers created with it have the problem of looking the same as other book covers. One author I know originally used the CreateSpace cover creator, but then got emails from fans alerting him that someone had "stolen" his cover, because someone else at CreateSpace opted for basically the same cover (different title, of course). If you want to try the cover creator tool, go ahead. It's possible they've made some improvements, and you'll get a cover you love. I just haven't had the best luck with it. Also remember that other books might have a nearly identical cover because they're getting the same choices as you are for fonts and images.

The next option, after making a cover yourself, is buying a pre-made cover. This is a great choice for self-publishers. You're getting high-quality covers made by graphic artists who understand how books in certain genres are supposed to look. Don't worry that the cover artist is getting rich by selling the same cover to several different authors. Typically, pre-made cover sites state that they only sell a cover once, so you won't see another book with the same cover as yours. If you don't find such a promise clearly stated on the website, feel free to email the designer and ask the site's policy on the issue.

When you search a pre-made site, the covers are usually separated by genre. That way, you know you're getting a cover that fits in your genre. Pre-mades can be purchased for as cheap as $35, but the mid-range level seems to be around $50 per cover. My first covers were pre-mades, and for my writer's group, I put together a small analysis of some pre-made sites I discovered. I looked over the list when writing this book. While some of the pre-made sites had gone out of business, many were still operating. My favorite pre-made site is http://goonwrite.com/. Some other sites include: Yocla Book Covers, http://yocladesigns.com/pre-made; Graphicz X Designs, http://graphiczxdesigns.zenfolio.com/f641008928; the Book Cover Designer, http://thebookcoverdesigner.com; Rocking Book Covers, http://www.rockingbookcovers.com/premade-covers; and Amygdala Designs, http://shop.amygdaladesign.net.

The final option for covers is commissioning one made just for your book. If you do this, you'll hire a graphic designer who will make your cover. It's typically cheaper if you select an image you want the designer to use. How do you find an image? Most designers will say on their website which companies they purchase stock images from, and direct you to select an image from that company. If the image you want to use is a personal image you own, they'll be willing to use that, too. However, if the image you own includes an identifiable person, they'll expect you to have a signed model release form. If you pay more, most designers will come up with a cover concept and images for you. Sites that offer pre-made covers usually offer custom designs too. That can add anywhere from $50 to $500 to the price you would pay for just a pre-made.

I really loved my cover designer for my book, *Third Life: Taken*. It was by Keri at http://www.alchemybookcovers.com/. I selected the image, and told Keri it needed to have a similar look and feel to previous covers in the series. The result was just what I wanted and only cost $50 (so it was cheaper than pre-mades at some other sites; I used the single-image "quick cover" option).

When you go to sites to purchase covers, you will often be given two options — the ebook cover and the print cover. The ebook cover is going to be the cheapest, as it includes only the front of the book. If you plan to publish a paperback copy of your book, you will need a cover that includes a front, spine, and back of the book. To get this cover, you can simply make a rear and spine to go along with your purchased ebook front cover, or you can pay an additional fee to your cover artist for the wraparound cover. Either way is acceptable. If you feel proficient at using software like Gimp or Photoshop, I would suggest doing the wraparound yourself and saving the money. You can do a wraparound as a solid color that matches one of the colors on the front of the cover. That way, you don't need a clean copy of the underlying image your cover artist used to make the front. Please note that you can't create the CreateSpace cover until your book's interior is complete. You will need the final page count before you can do the wraparound cover. You can purchase your ebook cover well in advance of the book's release, but you won't be able to make the wraparound yourself or send specs for it to the cover artist until later.

To create the wraparound cover yourself, download the cover template for a book your size. CreateSpace will want the trim size you've selected for your book (6x9 typically) and the number of pages in your book before you can download the template: https://www.createspace .com/Help/Book/Artwork.do. Open the template in your design software (CreateSpace provides the file types: PNG and PDF), and then import your front cover. You may need to adjust the size of the front cover slightly in order to get it to fit on the template. After importing the front cover, simply add color to the side and back. Be sure to leave the spot for the CreateSpace barcode blank. Add the back cover and spine text, and you're done. That was a pretty general overview. I've created a step-by-step tutorial with pictures, just for book purchasers: http://rjcrayton.com/sp/tutorials.

If you don't feel you can do the wraparound cover yourself, then pay the extra to get it from your cover artist. The wraparound cover often costs more than the ebook front (a front might cost $40, whereas the wrap is an extra $50 on top of the front fee). The reason the wrap-around costs more is because the cover designer needs to download the same CreateSpace template for your book size, which means there's a fair amount of customization to this piece.

Book Description (Blurb)

The book description, also called a blurb, is the next thing that readers will look at (and you have control over) to help them determine whether to buy your book or not. An interesting cover will lead the reader to click on the book and look at the description, so this is where you want to hook the reader so they choose to click, BUY NOW.

A good book description should be tantalizing and somewhat specific. Good book descriptions give enough information for the reader to be grounded in the story, but leave out enough that the reader wants to know what happens. In general, a book blurb should introduce the reader to the main character, state the main character's problem and then tell us what is at stake if the character doesn't solve his or her problem.

Like book covers, book descriptions vary slightly depending on the genre. In romance, for example, it's typical to have a book description that talks about the male and female lead characters (who will presumably fall in love). Often, the blurb talks about what the female lead wants in life, then talks about the male lead wants in life, then describes their meeting, and finally poses a question (something like, "Can this unlikely couple find love in the bowling lanes?") Here's a book description for an erotic title:

In this grown-up version of the famous fairy tale, Princess Adara is running from her old life and a forced betrothal. Adara wants love and passion, but knows she can't get them back home. When a raging storm halts her escape, Adara seeks refuge in the first dwelling she sees.

Prince Richard is tired of the trite, vain, frigid princesses his mother introduces him to in hopes he'll marry. On this stormy night, he's in the mood to love a woman, but he's all alone.

Adara arrives on the castle doorstep saying she's a princess in need of help. The queen is doubtful and decides to lock Adara in a room with a pea to determine if the girl is as royal as she claims. Richard believes the beautiful, charming stranger, but he wants her locked in a bedroom for other reasons.

When Richard and Adara hook up, there's more than a pea-sized bit of passion involved....

That's a typical blurb for that kind of a book.

Whatever genre you're writing in, spend some time on the book description and show it to people to get their opinions. Sometimes a second eye can spot something helpful. Book descriptions are going to be brief: just two to four short paragraphs. Don't get into too much minutiae or introduce too many characters. If you want some additional blurb writing tips, you can check out these two blog posts: The Art of the Blurb[6] and Book Description Basics[7].

Taglines

In addition to your book description, you may want to consider creating a catchy tagline you can use on Twitter or in other promotional material. The fabulous Laurie Boris had an awesome tagline for her book *Sliding Past Vertical*: "How long can a man carry a torch for a woman without getting burned?" The tagline is catchy and can be used in a variety of the marketing venues discussed in the marketing section.

* * *

Well, this wraps up Step 3 on polishing your book to professional. I know the section on blurb writing was short. However, my goal was to give you a flavor of the different ways to write blurbs. Unfortunately, blurb writing is something that lots of people struggle with and it's something that's only improved by reading lots of good blurbs and then crafting one yourself, getting feedback on it and honing it to perfection.

Once you've completed all the parts of Step 3, it's time to publish your book. You have your edited manuscript, cover, and description, which is all you'll need to upload your work to most sites. So, let's move on to Step 4.

---

[6] The Art of the Blurb, https://kjcharleswriter.wordpress.com/2013/09/06/the-art-of-the-blurb-how-to-write-back-cover-copy/

[7] Book Description Basics, http://www.indiesunlimited.com/2014/01/28/book-description-basics/

Step 3 Checklist

Editing

_____ Substantive editor (optional)

_____ Copy editor

_____ Proofreader (either hired or done yourself)

Cover

_____ Created or bought ebook front

_____ Wraparound cover (ordered for later or plan to make)

Blurb

_____ Blurb written

_____ Tagline written

STEP 4: PUBLISH

Now that your book content, cover, and description are ready, it's time to publish. When it comes to publishing, you have the option of electronic and print. Most self-publishers choose electronic, with many ignoring print all together. While a lot of the things we discuss in this step will apply to digital and print, we're going to discuss things in the context of digital self-publishing first. In Step 4, we're going to go over copyright registration, formatting your book, sales channels, pricing, keywords, and more.

Be advised: I'm going to discuss Amazon a lot in the Publish step, because Amazon is the largest ebook retailer. That does not mean I'm suggesting you only publish on Amazon. It just means that they're the model and if you figure out how to publish on the Amazon platform, you'll be able to figure out all the other platforms. Let's move on to the first part of the publishing process.

Copyright Registration

Copyright is a good place to start. While registering a copyright is an optional step, and I know many authors who don't do it, I recommend every publisher who is serious protecting their work register a copyright.

Why? Because, you can't sue somebody for copyright infringement (reproducing your book without permission) unless you register your copyright. I'm sure there are those of you who have heard that your work is copyrighted the moment you put it in tangible form (i.e. write it down). That is true. However, under United States law, you may not sue for infringement of that copyright unless you've actually registered your copyright with the US Copyright office. Below I've pasted the relevant sections from the US Copyright Office website, http://www.copyright.gov.

*Do I have to register with your office to be protected?

No. In general, registration is voluntary. Copyright exists from the moment the work is created. You will have to register, however, if you wish to bring a lawsuit for infringement of a U.S. work. See Circular 1, Copyright Basics, section "Copyright Registration."[8]

Why should I register my work if copyright protection is automatic?

Registration is recommended for a number of reasons. Many choose to register their works because they wish to have the facts of their copyright on the public record and have a certificate of registration. Registered works may be eligible for statutory damages and attorney's fees in successful litigation. Finally, if registration occurs within 5 years of publication, it is considered prima facie evidence in a court of law. See Circular 1, Copyright Basics, section "Copyright Registration" and Circular 38b[9], Highlights of Copyright Amendments Contained in the Uruguay Round Agreements Act (URAA), on non-U.S. works.

I've heard about a "poor man's copyright." What is it?

The practice of sending a copy of your own work to yourself is sometimes called a "poor man's copyright." There is no provision in the copyright law regarding any such type of protection, and it is not a substitute for registration.

Is my copyright good in other countries?

The United States has copyright relations with most countries throughout the world, and as a result of these agreements, we honor each other's citizens' copyrights. However, the United States does not have such copyright relationships with every country. For a listing of countries and the nature of their copyright relations with the United

---

[8] Circular 1, http://copyright.gov/circs/circ1.pdf
[9] Circular 38b, http://copyright.gov/circs/circ38b.pdf

States, see Circular 38a[10], International Copyright Relations of the United States.

(*Note: I am not infringing on the government's copyright by reprinting this. The US government releases most of its documents to the public domain, so you can generally republish instructions, papers, and other government-issued documents. In fact, before the Internet was so popular, several companies made money republishing government documents. However, do make sure that the document is public domain. The government contracts out certain documents, and the contractor retains the copyright. This law firm's website also offers an easy-to-understand Q&A on copyright registration.)

At the writing of this book, the fee for copyright registration was $35 for works with a single author and $55 for other works. As noted in the Q&A, you can register your work long after it's been published. The government considers registration within five years *prima facie* evidence that you are the creator of the work. *Prima facie* just means that it is presumed to be the truth unless somehow disproven. A person could actually register your work as their own (if you hadn't) and they'd be presumed the owner in court, and you'd have to go in and prove they lied to the copyright office when they registered the work (which is a serious crime). But, having the copyright gives you a leg-up if you ever face plagiarists.

How likely are people to copy your work? Probably not likely. The only cases that stand out in my mind are the one involving Rachel Anne Nune[11] and the one involving an erotica writer who was claiming [12]her own stories from websites where people posted their erotic shorts. The Nune story was still playing out when this book went to press, with Nune having sued her plagiarist[13]. Even though plagiarism is unlikely, the $35 is a minimal fee — a one-time cost that offers peace of mind.

The good news is if you have to sue, copyright infringement comes

---

[10] Circular 38a, http://copyright.gov/circs/circ38a.pdf

[11] Rachel Nune case, http://www.thepassivevoice.com/08/2014/standing-against-plagarism

[12] Erotica plagiarism case, http://www.npr.org/2012/01/29/146053943/on-amazon-an-uneasy-mix-of-plagiarism-and-erotica

[13] Nune sues plagiarist, http://rachelannnunes.blogspot.com/2014/10/plagiarism-timeline-shows-teacher-knew.html

with statutory damages if you win. Statutory damages mean the law, or statute, sets the damage amount. Statutory damages for copyright infringement could be as high as $150,000 per incident [14]of willful infringement. If for some reason you are not eligible for statutory damages (such as you waited too long to register your copyright), you can try to get actual damages. These are the actual damages the infringer caused you by copying your work. The court has to look at the infringer's records and your own, and then determine the financial damage that was actually caused you by the infringement. That could be nothing, or it could be a sum much less than $150,000, which is why people like statutory damages.

It generally takes the copyright office six months or longer to issue you a copyright certificate, but your official date of registration is listed as the day you submitted your application. You can apply using a paper form, but that costs more. It's most efficient to use the copyright office's electronic filing system at www.copyright.gov. I mentioned copyright first in this step, because I think it's important. Please note, however, that you can't actually submit your copyright application until the day you publish the book, unless you want to pay to pre-register your copyright. Pre-registering is more than three times the cost of a single author copyright, and is not recommended by the copyright office.

Front & Back Matter Formatting

In Step 3, you got your book pretty much ready for publication. However, there are a few additional things you'll have to add to your manuscript to make it a publishable book. These items are called the front and back matter. They go before and after your story. Some are required but most are optional. Here, I'll discuss several items you can potentially include in your front and back matter.

Front Matter (stuff before your book)

Copyright page. This page is required by all companies that publish books. The page only needs four words on it: Copyright YEAR YOUR NAME. That's it. So the copyright page for my book only needs to say: Copyright 2015 RJ Crayton. It's not uncommon to also include the words, "All rights reserved." These words are not necessary, however. The only thing your book must have to be published

---

[14] Statutory damages provisions, http://www.copyright.gov/title17/92chap5.html#504

on ebook sites is the Copyright and name. Some people use more elaborate copyright language, saying something like: "All rights reserved. This book or any portion thereof may not be reproduced or used in any manner whatsoever without the express written permission of the publisher except for the use of brief quotations in a book review." There's language that is even more extensive than that, and you're welcome to Google it and use it. However, the extra hyperbole and clarification are not necessary. People stealing your book disregard the copyright notice, whether it's brief or long.

Title Page. This is a single page with the title of your book and your author name. Most companies want you to include a Title Page. While readers should be familiar with the title based on the cover, it's just a second chance to reinforce this is the right book they're reading.

Active Table of Contents (TOC). This is not required, but I would advise it. When I say "active," I mean that it's hyperlinked to the actual chapters. So, when the user clicks Chapter 1, they're actually taken to Chapter One. If you're uploading directly to Amazon or Smashwords, you'll need to create your own active TOC. A nice feature of D2D is it will create an active TOC for you. The key thing is to use the same Microsoft Word Style (maybe Heading 2) for everything you want to be a TOC entry. The Smashwords Style Guide's explanation of how to create an active TOC seems to work for most companies, so using that one is a good idea. I won't repeat it here, because it's a copyrighted work to which I am not the copyright holder, but you can download the Style Guide at https://www.smashwords.com/books/view/52.

Subscribe to my mailing list. This is optional. A mailing list is a marketing tool that is used to send regular communication to readers. Mailing lists are a good way to let fans know when new books come out and are useful in marketing your book (we'll talk more about mailing lists in the Marketing section, p. 107). Some people suggest putting the "Subscribe to My List" page only in the back of your book. However, you can also put this in the front, so it's in the reader's mind even if they don't act on it. Then, when they get to the back of the book and see it again, they may be more prone to act. This page should include a hyperlink to a page where readers can sign up for the mailing list.

Dedication. If you'd like to dedicate your book to someone, this is traditionally placed in the front portion of the book on a page of its own. Dedications generally run only a sentence or two. If you would like to thank lots of people, such as your editor, friends, family or others, then you would put that in the acknowledgements section. While acknowledgements have traditionally been considered part of the front matter, along with the dedication, many publishers nowadays put them in the back of the book. As such, I will discuss acknowledgements in the Back Matter section.

Review Quotes. This is optional, too. Some people believe it helps to have great quotes from reviews of the book up front. See what I said? GREAT QUOTES. If the quotes from your review are ho hum, they shouldn't be highlighted. But, if you've got a few great quotes, feel free to stick them up front on a single page. You don't want too much front matter, so one page of good stuff is fine. Title the page something like, "What People are Saying about BOOK NAME."

What does a really good quote look like? You should know it when you see it, but I'll offer two that I use in promotional material for my book *Life First*:

"I really think RJ Crayton should be expecting calls for film rights, because this played out in my mind as I read it like a really great film…. It gripped you like King Kong and would not let go until you had finished the book."
-BestChickLit.com

"This novel was a poignant, riveting, thought provoking read that had me entranced from page one until the very end of the book. In simple speak, I literally could not put it down."
-Griffin's Honey Blog

A Word about Front Matter. I've listed a lot of things you can include in your front matter. I did that in order to show all the possibilities of items that can come in the front of the book. However, the copyright page, title page, and the active TOC are the only things that really must be at the front of your book, while the other things I've described can go as back matter. I would recommend using only one additional item to the three must-haves in the front of your book. The reason is you don't want your reader to have to turn through pages and pages of front matter to find the start of your book. Also, most ebook vendors (Amazon, Barnes and Noble, Google) offer a preview of your book. The preview ranges from 10 to 20 percent of the book's content. For shorter books, that front matter is going to eat into your 10 percent preview. You don't want a person to preview a copyright page, acknowledgements, review quotes, subscriber sign ups and never actually see text from a chapter. You want them to preview at least the beginning of the first chapter. I recommend using just a couple of things up front and everything else can go in the back. If you have a really short book, such as a children's book, there is a way to get Amazon to increase your book preview amount so readers see more than just the copyright page and TOC. Melinda Clayton discusses that method[15].

Back Matter

That was a lot of stuff in the front matter, right? So, you're thinking, how much more can there be? Not tons. Just a couple more things.

Book Preview. If you have another book out there, now is time to sell it. This should be the first thing the reader sees after they hit the end of your book. The next page should say: A FREE sneak preview of BOOK TITLE. Just like a reader will scan the first chapter in a bookstore, they'll scan the first chapter of this new book, just to see if it's as good as the one they just finished. This is your chance to hook the reader and get them to make an impulse purchase. Sneak previews tend to run 1 to 3 chapters, depending on how long each chapter is. At the end of the preview should be a link to the purchase page or the book's page on your own website (We'll talk about creating book pages on your website in the Marketing section). If the book is part of a series, the preview should be for the next book in the series. If the book is not part of a series, preview any title that readers of this one would likely enjoy. If you write romance and mysteries, preview mysteries for the mystery readers and romances for the romance readers. If this is your first novel, you won't have a book to preview. However, all subsequent novels should include some type of book preview.

Leave a Review. The best way to get reviews is to ask for them. Title this page, "Leave a Review," then follow that with a sentence or two asking readers who "enjoyed this book" to leave a review on the site where they purchased the book. While it would be lovely to put a link to the retailer's site so the reader could leave the review just like that, you can't put in a link unless you're distributing direct. With any

---

[15] Melinda Clayton article, http://www.indiesunlimited.com/2015/01/12/increasing-the-look-inside-preview-on-amazon/

book you've uploaded directly to that vendor's site, you'll link to the product page for your book at that vendor. If you've uploaded your book using a distributor (which sends your book to several vendors), you can suggest readers leave a review on your Goodreads Page (link to that) as well as the site where they purchased the book. (If you're unfamiliar with Goodreads, don't worry. I discuss it in Step 5.) Put the Leave a Review page immediately after your book ends.

Acknowledgements. This is the section where you thank the people who assisted you with the book. You often thank beta readers, editors, spouses, friends, agents, or anyone who you would like to acknowledge for their help in your publishing journey.

About the Author. This is your chance to tell the reader about you. I wouldn't get too cutesy. Just use your standard author bio. Haven't written a standard one yet? If that's the case, the author bio should first give the reader a quick snapshot of who you are. This snapshot should be relevant to your writing career — "Trixie Leggz is an erotic romance writer" or "John Eatsnailsforbreakfast writes hard-boiled crime novels." In the bio, you can also include your occupation, such as an investigative journalist, or a psychiatrist, if it is relevant to your writing. Occupation info is often useful to writers of nonfiction, as it gives their credentials. However, if you write psychological thrillers and you're a psychiatrist, you'll want to include that important credential in your bio. Next, you should talk about your writing achievements. You're the author of X number of books, or TITLE is your debut novel. Then, a little background. Prior to becoming an author, you did XYZ. Or you can skip that, and go into something somewhat fun and personable. When not writing, author loves to collect German dung beetles and play hopscotch with his kids. The last line of your bio should end with something like: To find out more about AUTHOR NAME, go to AUTHOR WEBSITE. Bam. That's it. You're done. If you still don't have the best feel for an author bio, go check out the bios of authors you like. See what they wrote, and if you like it, try to emulate it. If this is your first book, don't worry that you don't have a lot of book titles under your name. Nobody does when they begin writing. Focus on the positive attributes you have, and keep it short and simple. On the same page, just below your bio text, you can also list any social media sites where readers can find you, such as Twitter, Facebook, Tumblr, or Pinterest. (I'll be discussing social media more in the Marketing section).

Also By. This is a page where you list all the other books you've published. That way, readers who liked your book and said, "I'd love to read another of this author's books," will know where to find more. In an ebook, the other books listed should all be active hyperlinks the user can click and be taken to a page about the book. For any book you've formatted for a specific retailer (such as Amazon), you can put a direct link to that retailer's buy page. Your Amazon formatted book should contain links to your other books' Amazon pages. For any books you are using a distributor for, you'll need to put a link to the book page you created at your website. That book page should have buy links for all retailers. That way, if the same file is being distributed to Nook, Apple, and Kobo, the link is effective for each site.

Book Club Questions. If a book club decides to read your book, that's wonderful. One thing book clubs love when reading a book is to have ready-made discussion questions. If you think your book is the type a book club might like, then create some book club question and stick them in the back of your book. How do you go about creating book club questions? Glad you asked. I wrote an article on this for Indies Unlimited, and have included it in *Appendix D* (p. 185).

Even though we're still discussing mainly digital at this point, the front and back matter is essentially the same for the digital and print version of the book. The main difference is the digital versions will contain hyperlinks, whereas the print version will have the same text without the ability to hyperlink. The TOC in a print book will contain actual page numbers, rather than clickable links.

Banking, Emails

This is not a very complicated section. Very quickly, I thought I'd mention banking and email addresses, because we're about to discuss the different sales channels available to you. All the vendors require an email address and a location to send your money. For clarity in tracking your author earnings and author correspondence, consider creating a new bank account and email address for your author life.

Some people are hesitant to do this because it means another email account to check and another bank account to keep track of. However, there are some good reasons to start new for your author life.

In terms of the bank account, all vendors need a place to send the money you earn from your books. Most require a bank account number so they can direct deposit that income. Others only pay to PayPal accounts (Smashwords, for example). You'll need to have these accounts (PayPal or bank) set up in order to sell books online. Your books can't go live until the vendor has your payment information. If you want to have the author income automatically separated from your regular income (and easier to track when you file your tax returns), you can open a separate bank account. It also makes payments easier to track if you pay your author expenses (editors, cover artists, etc.) from that author account.

For people who are not familiar with PayPal, it is a company that allows you to pay people online from your checking account or a credit card. PayPal also allows you to accept payments. Generally, you will need to link your PayPal account to a checking account. PayPal is considered very safe, but some people have expressed discomfort about linking their checking account to the service. If that is you, then getting a separate author checking account to link to PayPal would be good for you. Even if you don't use a vendor that pays to PayPal, it's not a bad idea to open a PayPal account. Many of the advertisers that independent authors use get paid via PayPal.

If you open a new bank account for your author earnings, I don't recommend setting it up as a "business" account. Often, "business" accounts require more documentation of your business and business name, employees, incorporation documents, etc. Even though you're using it for business, it doesn't make a lot of sense to get a business account until you're making a lot of money. You can set up an account at your personal bank, or set up an account at an online bank. Online banks typically have fewer fees and pay higher interest rates. When you go set up your publishing accounts (next section: Digital Sales Channels, p. 48), you'll need to have two pieces of information from the bank: your account number and your routing number. For places that pay to PayPal, you'll need your PayPal email address.

Speaking of email addresses, you also may want to set up an email account specifically to handle your author correspondence. You can use a free service like Gmail or Yahoo to do this, or you can set up email via your website host. Any method is fine; it's up to you what you prefer. Setting up a separate account means you have to check an additional account. But, like a separate banking account, it offers you a dedicated space for author emails. You don't have to worry that an important author email got lost in the oodles of spam you get at your personal email account.

I would strongly encourage people to use a separate email for their author presence. You will be corresponding with fans, possibly from this address, and it's possible it might get posted on some public venues. If you don't want your personal email that your friends and family use out in the public sphere, it's best to get an author account email address.

Digital Sales Channels

Now that you've added front and back matter, decided whether to get a copyright (hopefully yes), and opened any additional banking or email accounts that you want, you can look at where you want to publish your book. We're only going to look at digital sales channels right now, as most self-publishers make their money in ebooks. We'll discuss print a little later.

In terms of online vendors, there are many places to publish your book. I'm going to discuss eight sales channels and two distributors for digital (and three more when it comes to print). Because there are so many, it can feel a bit overwhelming. The key thing to remember with sales channels is that they are the way readers find your books. You're going to pick your sales channels to align with your goals. If you want the opportunity to reach the most readers, you could upload your book to all the sales channels. If you just want a book published, it might not be worth the headache to you to publish on all these channels.

In the sales channel section, I'm going to discuss each sales channel briefly. The components that are probably of most interest to you are going to be the areas where each sales channel differs from the others. I will note the royalty rate authors get paid on each sales channel, which ereading devices the site works with, and whether the site has any special attributes or reaches a niche market.

I'll spend the most time discussing Amazon because Amazon is the biggest market. It also has a system that's similar to the others, so if you understand how it works, you'll have an idea of what to expect from other retailers. The goal of the Sales Channels section is to help you understand what your options are, not for you to understand each option in 100 percent detail. This is an overview, and if you want to know more about a vendor, feel free to click through to the site.

A quick note on ereading devices. People who read a lot often prefer a dedicated ereader, rather than reading books on a tablet or phone. Ereaders tend to be proprietary. Amazon's Kindle will only (easily) read books sold via Amazon. The Nook will only (easily) read books sold via Barnes and Noble. People who know what they're doing can convert their book files for either, but the average customer will buy via the site that easily gets books onto their devices. The two primary ebook formats are mobi, which Kindle uses, and epub, which most other ereaders use. Ebooks can also be read in computer-friendly file formats, such as text (TXT), rich text format (RTF), and portable document format (PDF). Most ereaders can also read text and PDF files.

Amazon. Most authors, myself included, sell the most books via Amazon. I think it's wise for all authors to publish on Amazon.

Amazon offers two publishing options: KDP[16] (Kindle Direct Publishing) and KDP Select[17]. KDP is Amazon's main digital publishing. With KDP, you are the publisher, and you get to keep all the royalties for your books. Amazon royalty rates[18] vary depending on the price of your book. If your book costs less than $2.99 or more than $9.99, the royalty rate is 35 percent (so, on a 99 cent book, you'd earn 35 cents). Amazon has decided they don't want books priced too high or too low. So, if you're hoping to earn a bigger cut, books should be priced between $2.99 and $9.99, which gives you a 70 percent royalty rate.

While KDP refers to Amazon's self-publishing program, people sometimes mistakenly use KDP to refer to KDP Select. Select and KDP are different. Select requires you to agree to **sell your ebooks exclusively** on Amazon.com. You can still sell the print version of the books on all retailers (and many people do, using Amazon's CreateSpace), but the only digital version of your book is on Amazon. You may include digital samples (10 percent or less) on your own website or a sample site (such as Wattpad), but Amazon has to be the only place people can get the whole book. Select is not a permanent program. When you enroll in Select you agree to be exclusive for a 90-day period. At the end of the period, you may re-enroll or opt out of the program.

Why would an author choose to be exclusive to Amazon? In return,

---

16 KDP, https://kdp.amazon.com/

17 KDP Select, https://kdp.amazon.com/help?topicId=A6KILDRNSCOBA

18 Amazon royalty rates, https://kdp.amazon.com/help?topicId=A301WJ6XCJ8KW0

Amazon gives Select authors a couple of things that non-Select authors don't get. If you're in Select, you have the ability to make your book free for five days, and then go back to regular price. We'll talk about free more in the marketing strategies section, but many authors like the ability to run the book free so they can garner some fans willing to take a chance on an unknown author.

If you don't like the idea of making your price free, joining KDP Select allows you to lower your 70 percent royalty item to a 35 percent royalty price and still get a 70 percent royalty. This is called a Kindle Countdown Deal[19]. You can drop your $4.99 book to 99 cents and take 70 percent on the 99 cents, rather than just 35 percent. The other thing you get with the countdown deal is that buyers know your price is lower. During a countdown deal, Amazon will put a line through your regular price (say $4.99) and indicate your new price. If you are not part of Select and choose to lower your price for a sale, the buyer just thinks the price was always the lower price. There is nothing to indicate that the buyer is getting a deal.

Being in Select also lets you put your book in Amazon's borrowing programs. The first borrowing program is called the Kindle Online Lending Library[20] (KOLL). This program allows Amazon Prime users to borrow one book each month, which they read at no cost, but you as the author are paid for. The other program is Kindle Unlimited[21] (KU). This program allows users to borrow an unlimited number of books each month (10 at a time, but no limit to how many they ultimately read). For KU reads to count as a borrow, the user must finish 10 percent of the book. KOLL borrows always count as a borrow, regardless of the percentage of the book read.

Books that are borrowed, either through KU or KOLL, are not paid at your list price. They are paid at a price set by Amazon from its "Global Fund." The rates paid vary each month, and have been as high as $2.51 per borrow, but had dropped to $1.37 in January of 2015 (it had been as low as $1.33 in October 2014).

Indie authors have complained about some of the program's components. For example, many are unhappy that books priced 99 cents

---

[19] Kindle Countdown Deal, https://kdp.amazon.com/help?topicId=A2MJTCAY-TCBNW2
[20] KOLL, https://kdp.amazon.com/help?topicId=A3BQJE2QV37M1B
[21] KU, https://kdp.amazon.com/help?topicId=AA9BSAGNO1YJH

get the higher payment when they're borrowed. Others have complained about the 10 percent read requirement for KU, contending Amazon doesn't care how much buyers read, so it shouldn't care how much borrowers read. Others have complained that the KU model discourages user buys. It's not clear if Amazon will try to address these complaints and make changes to the program, but before you sign up, do check the parameters, in case any changes have been made.

Amazon is the only retailer that offers perks for being exclusive to its site. Ebooks sold via Amazon are formatted in the mobi file type. Amazon works with the Kindle ereader. The Kindle reading app allows users of most computers and Apple or Android-based mobile products (mobile phone or tablet) to read the books on those devices. Kindle also reads PDFs.

Other Retailers

Amazon is the big fish when it comes to ebook sales, but there are other vendors out there. You'll find a handful of authors who make most of their money somewhere other than Amazon. I've seen a woman post online that the Google Play store was her biggest seller. Others do well at Barnes and Nobles, while others do well at Kobo.

At the end of this chapter, I'll give you my thoughts on what you should do when you start publishing (go into Select or go to the other retailers as well). For the moment, let's just take a look at the other digital marketplaces where you can sell your books. I am including seven below.

Barnes and Noble. The site for the brick-and-mortar bookstore sells ebooks. A lot of them. It's at Barnesandnoble.com or Nook.com. You can publish directly with them by going to www.nookpress.com and signing up. They don't have any particularly robust author programs or even author pages. But, ereaders are proprietary. If someone bought a Nook as their ereader, they can't buy books from Amazon. One way to get those customers is to be in the Barnes and Noble online store. Barnes and Noble ebooks are formatted as Nook's proprietary format, which is based on epub. Ebooks sold at Barnes and Noble can be read on the Nook. Like Amazon, Nook offers an app that allows users of computers and Apple and Android-based mobile products to read Nook books on those devices. Nooks read epub and

PDF files. The royalty rates[22] for Barnes and Noble are 65 percent for books priced $2.99-$9.99; 40 percent for books priced less than $2.98 or more than $10. The minimum price you can set at Barnes and Noble is 99 cents.

iBooks/iTunes. This is Apple's bookstore, and anyone with an i-product (iPhone, iMac, iPad) or Apple device is going to have access to it. To upload to this site directly, go to this site for instructions, http://www.apple.com/itunes/working-itunes/sell-content/books/book-faq.html. You can only upload via this site using Apple machine (don't worry if you don't have an Apple computing product; most people use a distributor to deal with Apple. We're going to talk distributors in the next section, p. 57). Owners of Apple products are going to be the purchasers using this system, as it's one of the default stores for users of those products. Apple uses the epub and proprietary .books format. It's unlikely anyone but Apple product users will be purchasing from this store. Apple pays 70 percent royalties on book sales, regardless of your price. Apple's royalty rates are not listed publicly online. You have to register as a vendor before you can see them.

Google Play. Yes, Google's app store also sells books. Lots of them. You have to upload directly to Google Play (most distributors don't upload to them). Unfortunately, the Google Play interface is confusing and reading the sales report is a nightmare. With most vendor sites, you can view your sales numbers online once you have logged into their system with your username and password. With Google Play, you have to download a new report to your computer every time you want to see new sales numbers. For some reason, the sales report is often a day or two behind, as well. Most vendors offer same day sales reporting, with a few hours of lag. However, some people say they sell a lot of books on Google Play. Here's the site to go to for Google Play uploading: https://play.google.com/books/publish. Google Play offers ebooks as either PDFs or epub files. PDFs can be read by any device with a PDF reader (including phones and tablets). Similarly, epubs can be read on any device with an app that reads epubs. Nook, Sony, and smaller label ereaders can read Google Play ebooks. The Google royalty rate is 52 percent. I talk about digital book pricing later, but *please note that the Google Play store regularly lowers the*

---

[22] Barnes & Noble royalty rates, http://cp-barnesandnoble.kb.net/kb/?ArticleId=4377&source=Article&c=12&cid=28#tab:homeTab:crumb:7:artId:4259

prices authors set. Some authors choose not list at Google Play because of it. In the Digital Pricing section (p. 64), I discuss this issue in more detail.

Smashwords. Primarily a distributor, Smashwords also has a store. In this section, I am discussing Smashwords as a store only. (I'll discuss it as a distributor in the distributor section). The Smashwords store sells ebooks only, and one nice thing is that you can generate coupons readers can use to purchase your book at a discount. On Amazon, if you want to give a review copy, you actually have to pay the cost of the book (full price taken from your pocket; Amazon gets its cut, then the rest goes back into your pocket in two months when Amazon pays you. Not ideal). With Smashwords, you can use coupon codes to offer up to 100 percent off your books. It's a great way to give review copies or to give fans a discount without changing the price at all your retailers. Find them at http://www.smashwords.com. Smashwords publishes its ebooks in the widest array of formats: RTF, TXT, PDF, epub, and mobi. If a person has a device on which they wish to read digitally, they can find a compatible format on Smashwords. The royalty rate[23] for the Smashwords store is 85 percent. (Please remember, this is the store only; When distributed via Smashwords, you will earn less than 85 percent. See the Distributors section for details, p. 57.)

Kobo. This online retailer is more popular in Europe and Canada than it is in the US. When there was a large dustup in Great Britain over pornography titles showing up in search results for seemingly innocuous phrases like "Daddy's little girl," Kobo was one of the first to purge titles[24]. This was because Kobo is widely used in Great Britain, the source of the uproar. I don't personally know anyone who sells a lot through Kobo, but you always find one or two people on an author board saying how Kobo is their big source of revenue. Learn more at http://www.kobo.com/writinglife. Kobo sends files in epub, and works primarily with its own proprietary Kobo reader. The Kobo reader can read epub and PDF files. For books that are original content, Kobo pays[25] 70 percent royalties for titles priced $2.99 and above

---

[23] Smashwords royalty rate, https://www.smashwords.com/about/support-faq#GettingStarted

[24] Kobo purges titles, http://www.ibtimes.co.uk/kobo-wh-smith-closes-self-publishing-indecent-514006

[25] Kobo royalty rates, http://download.kobobooks.com/writinglife/Kobo/en-US/KWL-User-Guide.pdf

and a 45 percent royalty on all other titles. If you have chosen to reproduce a public domain work and list it on Kobo, the royalty rate is only 20 percent, regardless of the price.

All Romance Ebooks. If you're doing romance or erotica, this is a great place to be. People who write any form of romance say they sell a fair amount on this site, so I would definitely recommend it for that genre. If your book is slightly romantic or has some romantic moments, you can also consider placing it on this site, as the romance is broken into categories that include crime, thriller, suspense, sci-fi, fantasy, and steampunk. So, if romance is a strong secondary element, consider placing here. You can set up a publisher account at https://www.allromanceebooks.com/publishers.html. All Romance Ebooks offers files in mobi, epub, or PDf, and readers can select the file format they wish to read in. Self-published authors sign up as publishers and earn 60 percent of sales price[26].

Libiro. This site popped up as a standalone place to sell books, offering a higher royalty rate than Amazon (75 percent). I can't say that most consumers know about it, but it is a place you can sell your books. Find out more at http://www.libiro.com/index.php?route=information/information&information_id=9. Libiro offers files in epub or PDF. It works with any reader or app that can access those files.

Formatting for Different Vendors

Those were a lot of sites and each has its own formatting requirements. Most of them are based on a person starting with a Microsoft Word file and the site converting that to the required ebook format. The site with the most stringent requirements is Smashwords. It calls its ebook converter Meatgrinder. Next, in terms of formatting requirements, are Amazon and Nook. The one with the least requirements is Draft2Digital (D2D), a distributor that tries to make it easy on authors. Most formatting can be done by an author who wants to spend some time on it. However, if you and computers are like mixing oil and water, you can hire a formatter to get your manuscript ready for publication. Amazon, Nookpress, Smashwords, and D2D all accept a Microsoft Word file formatted to their specs. Apple, Google Play, Libiro, and All Romance Ebooks all want a document already in an ebook format. Most want epub, but a couple want several different formats

---

[26] All Romance ebooks royalty rate, http://www.allromanceebooks.com/faq-2.html

(epub, mobi, or PDF).

How do you get the mobi and epub files for other sites? There are a couple of options. First, you can download and use the free software, Calibre (http://calibre-ebook com). That will convert documents for you with minimum hassle. If you are distributing on Smashwords or D2D, you can simply use the final epub or mobi documents they create for you. Those files don't list any specific retailers in them, so they're easy to distribute to places that require those file types. Smashwords used to require you put "Smashwords Edition" in the front matter of its files, but dropped that requirement in 2014.

If you decide to format the document yourself using a Microsoft Word file, several sellers have guides explaining how to format your book for conversion to ebook. Below, I'm including a link to those guides. If you don't think you'll be able to follow the steps in the guide, you're welcome to hire an ebook formatter. I recommend using the guides to do the formatting in Microsoft Word, because you will better be able to update your book. Every time you publish a new book, you have to go and update the back matter (Other Books By, About the Author) of all your other books. You want to be able to do that yourself, rather than having to hire a formatter to fix each book for you.

Smashwords Style Guide
https://www.smashwords.com/books/view/52

Building Your Book for Kindle
https://kdp.amazon.com/help?topicId=A2MB3WT2D0PTNK

Nookpress Style Guide
http://cp-barnesandnoble.kb.net/kb/article?ArticleId=4339 &source=Article&c=12&cid=28

Draft2Digital Style Guide
https://www.draft2digital.com/styleguide/

Indie Author Group Service Providers (to hire a formatter)
https://www.facebook.com/notes/indie-author-group/service-providers-publishing-support/853301738035805 (Look for formatters.)

File Names. I thought I'd add in a quick note about file names here to help you keep organized. When you are finished with a book, save the book as BookNameDATE. So, my book *Life First* has a version saved as LifeFirst20130618. The date is written as year first, then month, then day. In the example I just gave, that's the version of Life First published on June 18, 2013. Every time I change the file, say to update the Also By section, I change the date to the current date. If you save your files this way, you will easily be able to figure out which is the most current version of your manuscript. If you download the epub version of your file from D2D, immediately add the date to the name so you know when you downloaded it. This should keep you from accidentally uploading an older version of the file, or sending a reviewer an old file that perhaps has an error a reader pointed out and you later fixed. At some point, you can purge old files. As a practical matter, though, I've found people tend not to purge older files, so it's best to have a way of distinguishing older versions from newer ones.

Preview Your Content. All the sites (Amazon, Smashwords, D2D, NookPress) that convert your Microsoft Word document into an ebook file (mobi, epub, or PDF) allow you to preview your document before making the ebook live on the site. Do that. Some, like Amazon and NookPress, have a browser-based previewer so you can see what your book looks like right there in your web browser. Other sites require you to download the file and look at it on your computer. If you have to download the file, you can only view it if your computer has the right software. If you downloaded Calibre to create ebook files, then that software should open both epub and mobi files. If you don't have Calibre, you can download the Kindle Reading software (https://www.amazon.com/gp/digital/fiona/kcp-landing-page?ie =UTF8&ref =kcp_pc_mkt_lnd) to check out your mobi file, or OverDrive (https://www.overdrive.com/) to check out your epub file. All of these are free downloads.

When you preview your document, you want to first check the Table of Contents and make sure it works accurately. When you click the Chapter 1 link, does it actually take you to Chapter 1? You need to do this for all the linked TOC items. This might take a few minutes if you write a genre where short chapters are common (I had 62 chapters in my first novel, a thriller), but it's important to look through the book the way a reader would and make sure internal and external hyperlinks work. Also glance at the pages of each chapter for any formatting errors that jump out at you. For example, I often offset section breaks with three asterisks centered on the page. On a scroll through, you might notice that one set of asterisks is left aligned. If you find errors in the preview, jot them down (include the error and the chapter in which it appears). After you finish reviewing the preview file, go fix errors in your Word Document, then re-upload and view the new preview. If all the errors are fixed and you haven't noticed new ones, you can approve the file for publication.

Distributors, Libraries, and Subscription Services

There are many formatting guidelines that you could have to follow for your documents, if you want to have your book available at all the retailers. In theory, you would have to create a version of your book that met each site's formatting requirements. Well, if you went to each site, you would. Luckily there are companies out there that are distributors. They take one version of your file and upload it to the various sites, per the site's requirements. You manage changes for all those sites via the distributor. Once you have multiple books, the primary advantage of a distributor become really clear — easy changes to the back matter. With the publication of each new book, you have to go and change the Also By section for all the previous books (so that section includes your newest book). With a distributor, you change one file, and the distributor will send the update to all the retailers selling the book. If you have to make this change at each site, that could triple your workload. For example, if you have published 10 books, and are now publishing the 11th, you would need to go change the Also By section for the previous 10 books. That's enough work in and of itself. Now, go do it for your Barnes and Noble version, your Apple version, your Kobo version, and all the others. It's not complicated, but it does mean a decent amount of extra time.

Most indie authors upload directly to Amazon and use distributors for the other retailers. There are actually several places you can use to distribute your book, but most of the lesser known ones charge you a fee for the privilege and take a commission to boot. The two primary distributors for ebooks that have no upfront fees and simply charge a commission are Smashwords and Draft2Digital. Let's take a quick minute to discuss each.

Smashwords

Smashwords has been around the longest and has the most distribution offerings. However, many people, myself included, have found Smashwords to be incredibly slow in making changes. I once requested a price change to occur at one of the retailers and it took 23 days for it to happen. My book was on sale for 99 cents for roughly 15 days longer than I'd wanted it to be on sale. (I knew Smashwords could lag a bit, so I put in my request about a week prior to when I actually needed the price changed. And it still didn't happen.) So, there's a real problem with pushing out data and making changes to your books. It doesn't happen with every retailer. Personally, I've had very good luck with changes made to Apple and Kobo. However, changes sent to Barnes and Noble often didn't get done without a lot of back-and-forth between me and Smashwords. On the plus side, Smashwords, in addition to being a distributor, is a store. As I mentioned in the Digital Sales Channels section, this is great because the store lets you generate coupon codes for free or discounted copies of your ebooks.

Smashwords also has wider reach than any other distributor. In addition to Barnes and Noble, Apple, and Kobo, Smashwords distributes to the Oyster subscription service, OverDrive (which provides ebooks to most libraries), and ScribD. If you'd like a shot at having your book in a library's electronic system, you probably want to do Smashwords' OverDrive distribution.

When you upload a book to Smashwords, it automatically goes to the Smashwords store. However, if you want it distributed to other vendors, it must pass through Meatgrinder, the company's manuscript vetting system. Meatgrinder requires you to make sure your document is properly formatted, and there is a free ebook that explains how to format your document for Meatgrinder. Formatting for Meatgrinder takes time and attention to detail, but it's not inherently difficult. You just have to allot the time to sit down and do it. If you are distributing to several locations, it's probably best to format your document for Meatgrinder first, as it has the most stringent requirements. Then use the document you sent to Meatgrinder as the base for your other formats.

Smashwords makes its money by charging a commission on books sold. When authors sell direct via the Smashwords store, the royalty rate is 85 percent of list price. When authors sell through a distributed site (such as Barnes and Noble), the rate will vary (https://www.smashwords.com/about/supportfaq#Royalties). For many vendors, authors earn 60 percent of list price (which is less than you would earn if you went directly to the vendor site). If you are selling a small number of books, the percentage paid to Smashwords is generally a fair exchange for not having to upload books directly. However, if you start selling hundreds or thousands of books monthly via a specific site you distribute to through Smashwords, it's probably worth moving to a direct relationship with that vendor. Again, to use Smashwords, go to http://www.smashwords.com.

Draft2Digital

D2D, as it is known, is the new kid on the block. They distribute to Barnes and Noble, Kobo, and Apple. D2D is known for being fast and communicative. When you talk to other authors, the big difference between Smashwords and D2D is that the company is quick and efficient. Personally, I've had great experience with the titles I've published through D2D. The company sends you an email when your book has been distributed to a vendor. That email includes a link where you can see your book live on the site. D2D is also extremely communicative. In November, the site sent an email explaining when each of its vendors (Barnes and Noble, Apple, Kobo) would be closed for Christmas, and how much lead time authors would need to make changes and have them go into effect prior to those closures. Additionally, my titles appeared on most vendor sites within 48 hours, which is much quicker than I've ever had distribution through Smashwords. D2D gets paid the same way as Smashwords, by taking a percentage of sales. That percentage is 10 percent of list price (https://www.draft2digital.com/faq/#faq-category-pricing). Like I said with Smashwords, if you find you're moving a lot of books via a particular site, it is probably worth moving to a direct relationship with that vendor so you're not losing 10 percent on each sale. To find out more about D2D, go to https://www.draft2digital.com.

Vendors to Distribute to Directly

Please note that you should create direct vendor accounts at Amazon, the Google Play Store, All Romance Ebooks, and Libiro. Neither D2D nor Smashwords distribute to Google Play All Romance, or Libiro. A few small distributors who charge $199 for the privilege will send your title to the Google Play store, but I don't think it's worth the cost. While Smashwords distributes to Amazon, it's a very limited distribution, and most people recommend going directly to Amazon. If most of your sales come from Amazon, it's best to have direct, up-to-date access to the sales data and to be able to make changes quickly. Publishing direct to Amazon also lets you change your keywords and categories (which we'll talk more about shortly). Amazon accepts a Microsoft Word document for upload. Google Play Store, All Romance Ebooks, and Libiro all request an epub or PDF version of your file. You can actually just use the file you created at Smashwords or D2D as the file you upload to sites that require epub. Smashwords used to require authors to include the words "Smashwords Edition" on all ebooks sold via the distributor, but they got rid of that requirement. You can download your epub or PDF file from your Smashwords book page (while you are logged in; under "Download the full version of this book") or your Draft2Digital book page (on the right hand side, you'll seen an orange "Download File" button — the text is red).

Creating Vendor Accounts

Amazon. When you publish through KDP, you need to sign up for their service. If you want, you can use the same Amazon account you use to make purchases for your publishing account. Just go to http://kdp.amazon.com and log in using your current username and password. If you would like a separate account for your publishing account, you can simply go to the KDP website and click, "Sign Up." Then, you'll need to sign up with an email address that is different from your other Amazon account (Amazon only allows one account per email address). Before you can publish your book, you'll need to fill in banking information and personal information (legal name, address, and social security number). You have the option of using an employer ID number (EIN) instead of an SSN, but most people don't apply for a government-issued EIN to self-publish.

To publish a new book, you'll click on the "Bookshelf" page (at the top of the screen) and then click on "Add New Title." Follow the Amazon instructions, and you'll be fine for adding your content, which will include your formatted document, your book cover (JPG or TIFF file), book blurb (product description), keywords, and pricing information (see VAT section below for additional note on pricing).

Other Vendors. The other vendors generally have a similar setup. Instructions are fairly straightforward, so if you follow them, you should be fine. One thing to note with Smashwords is that you will need to select which vendors you want to publish your book with. Once you've logged in, you select the sites to distribute your book to through the Channel Manager[27]. Using radial buttons, you'll select "Distribute" or "Opt Out" for the various vendors. Be sure to opt out of Amazon, as you want to publish direct there. Also opt out of any other vendors you're not interested in.

VAT. In 2015, Europe changed the way VAT (value added taxes) were collected on ebooks. It is incredibly complicated to understand and apply, however, most vendor sites will do it for you. Check the box that allows them to configure the VAT for your titles. Please note that Amazon has a policy of price-matching. This means they guarantee customers they will match the lowest price out there. Some sites, including Smashwords, give you the option of not adding VAT to your titles. You simply pay the tax yourself from your share of your book's profits. Someone might do this to make their book appear cheaper compared to other titles. However, if you do this and you are also selling at Amazon, Amazon will price-match your book so it's cheaper on Amazon's site. Be aware of that if you choose not to let the vendors make your price VAT inclusive.

Categories & Keywords

Categories and keywords are used to help categorize your books so readers can find them. Categories are the equivalent of genre. In the online world, categories tell you where your book belongs — mystery, thriller, romance, etc. Keywords are a little trickier, but they essentially help route readers to your books. They're a descriptive term attached to your book, so that when readers search for a specific type of book (say, they want a "doctor romance"), your book pops up. Again, keywords are tricky, and we'll go into a little more detail after we flesh out categories.

When you go to vendor sites and begin filling in the information needed to publish your book, all sites will ask for your book's BISAC (Book Industry Standards and Communications) categories. These are equivalent to genres. BISAC categories drill down, getting more specific the deeper down you go. Initially, you will only be given the choice of two categories: Fiction and Nonfiction. Once you select Fiction,

---

[27] Channel Manager, https://www.smashwords.com/dashboard/channel-Manager/

you'll be given the choice of several subcategories, such as erotica, mystery, romance, science fiction, and thriller. Most places use the BISAC categories as a starting place, including Amazon. This is the list of current BISAC categories: https://www.bisg.org/bisac-subject-codes. Check it out if you'd like to see your category options. You'll want to pick a category that fits your book, as readers will be disappointed if you classify your book as Political fiction (because it involves a senator), but has very little politics in it, and focuses almost entirely on the senator's romance with an actress. That work might be better classified under Contemporary Romance. If you're unsure what category you should be in, go check out what books appear in the categories on the vendor's site. See if your book would fit right in or be an outlier. Each vendor site has a way to see books in broad categories. I'll use Amazon as an example here. Go to their list of Best Sellers, and look on the left side of your screen. That is the list of top-level categories books fall into. Click on any of them and you'll see lower level categories beneath them. Please note that when picking categories on Amazon, you may only be able to select a top-level category to appear in, and you may need to use keywords to get your book into the more specific category.

This seems like a good place to segue into keywords. On most vendor sites, after you've selected a category, they will ask you for keywords. (Not all do. Google Play, even though it's the product of search engine giant Google, is remarkably devoid of a place to attach keywords to your book). The keywords are designed to help readers search the buying site. Your keywords should be something you think people who are interested in buying your books will search. So, if your book is about boy scouts on a camping trip, you might use "boy scout camping" as a keyword. You probably noticed that was an entire phrase, not just a single word. Phrases are fine, and as long as the phrase is separated from your next keyword by a comma, it will count as a single keyword.

The reason I say keywords are tricky is because they require reverse engineering. You have to guess what you think people who are interested in your book are using as search terms. It's an inexact art, and there are entire posts[28], devoted to keywords. Author Nicholas Stephenson, who runs the website http://www.yourfirst10kreaders.com/, markets a system that suggests authors find keywords that drive

---

[28] Keyword post, http://www.kboards.com/index.php/topic,205816.0.html

readers to their books on Amazon. When done correctly, keywords will help your book turn up in the top of the search results when a customer searches that topic. If you are at or near the top of that search, you'll improve book sales. You're welcome to check out the Kboards post as well as Stephenson's free videos on his site (you must join his mailing list to access the videos). Keywords are hard to master, so don't expect instant fluency. Do the best you can, and know that you can always tinker with them later (We'll talk more about tinkering in Step 7).

Whether you check out the aforementioned or not, just remember that keywords are one gateway that brings readers to your books, so they should be relevant. Keywords, unfortunately, are limited. Amazon allows seven keywords separated by commas. If your book is a historical fiction about Mary, Queen of Scots', romance with Francis II, King of France, then you might include "royal romance" as a keyword.

In addition to helping readers find your books in a search, keywords on Amazon can help get your books into the right category. Amazon has categories that are more detailed than the BISAC ones. To get into those categories, you need to use keywords. As an example, Amazon has a subcategory in Young Adult Horror called Angels & Demons. You can't select that as a category when you upload your book. The only way to get on Amazon's YA Horror Angels & Demons category is to use angel as a key word. Amazon lists the key words you need to get into certain categories: https://kdp.amazon.com/help?topicId=A200PDGPEIQX41.

Why are these categories important? Because Amazon has lots of bestseller lists and it ranks bestsellers for every subcategory. If there are readers obsessed with cyberpunk, they're going to go to the sci-fi section, click on cyberpunk, and look at the best sellers in only that category. If your book is cyberpunk, you'd like to be on that list. Because Amazon has so many categories, it's easier to get on a category bestseller list, rather than the overall bestseller list. To be atop the cyberpunk category, you may only need an Amazon sales rank of 20,000 (meaning you're the 20,000[th] best-selling book on Amazon.com). To get such a ranking, you'd need to be selling 5-15 books per day. Author Teresa Ragan has a handy sales-rank to books-sold conversion chart here: http://www.theresaragan.com/salesrankingchart.html.) If your book is on the first page of a category best seller list, it is more likely to be seen and purchased by buyers. So getting your keywords right is important to selling the book.

Digital Pricing

Book pricing isn't rocket science, but there are some things you should consider when deciding how to price your ebook.

Minimums. Some ebook vendors have a minimum price you can sell your book for. If you upload directly to Amazon (recommended) or NookPress (not recommended), the minimum price you can set is 99 cents. I know that people offer their books for free on Amazon and Barnes and Noble, but they can't achieve that by setting the price that way when they upload the book. (I'll discuss how to make a book free in the *Marketing section,* p. 101.) Other sites, such as Google Play and Apple, allow you to set the price of your book as free.

Length. How long is your book? Full length novels (50,000+) generally go for more than shorter works, such as novellas and short stories. Novellas (10,000-40,000) or short stories (> 10,000) might sell for 99 cents, while a full-length novel could sell for $2.99-$4.99, depending on the genre.

Genre. Believe it or not, some genres command higher prices than other. Erotica, for whatever reason, sells at a higher price point than most fiction. So, erotica writers often price novellas (10k-20k word pieces) for $2.99. I've seen some erotica writers sell a 7,000 word piece for $2.99. However, for many genres, you can't sell books with such small word counts at that price. Nonfiction also tends to be higher priced than fiction. Any book that is heavy in graphics, such as a graphic novel or photography, is going to sell for a higher price. This is because the file size is much larger, and some vendors charge authors more to distribute books with large file sizes.

Series Order. We talked briefly about series before. If you have several books in a series, you generally price the introductory book cheaper, as a loss-leader, and sell subsequent books at a higher price. Book one might be 99 cents, or even free, while books two, three, or four could be priced $2.99, $3.99, and $4.99; or they could be priced all $3.99. But often you'll have a progression.

Dead Zone. Mark Coker, who started Smashwords, did an ebook pricing survey to find out what the typical ebook price was. Like Amazon, he discovered that $2.99 was the most common price, and that indie authors did well pricing between $2.99 and $4.99. However, he noted that $1.99 was the dead zone — or black hole — of book sales. People did not sell very many books at that price, and the profit was middling. On Amazon, you're in the 35 percent royalty bracket, but you're not getting volume to make up for the lower royalty, as you might get at 99 cents. The Coker study is here: http://blog.smash-words.com/2013/05/new-smashwords-survey-helps-authors.html.

Google Play Store. The store is hotly debated among indie authors because of its policy of slashing prices the publisher sets. I suspect this is why most distributors don't distribute to the Google Play Store. Essentially, if you price your book at $2.99, Google will slash the book's price to $2.09. Google Play still pays the author 52 percent of the list price. However, because one vendor, Amazon, price-matches, Google's unauthorized price dropping has a horrible ripple effect, and the book's price at Amazon will likely get lowered. Amazon does not pay royalty based on list price. It pays royalty based on the price it is on the site. So if Amazon drops the $2.99 price to $2.09, the author gets paid the royalty on the $2.09 price. (Also, for a book at that price, the royalty rate drops from 70 percent to 35 percent). Authors who experienced this were not happy. There is a fix. This author suggests pricing guidelines[29] for uploading to Google Play. OK, problem solved you say. Not quite. A couple of authors have reported that Google decided to give their book away for free (and still pay them the royalty), but this caused Amazon to price-match their book to free (and Amazon does not give authors royalties on books priced free). Here are the incidents, as self-reported by the authors on the Kboards site: Author One, http://www.kboards.com/index.php/topic,187263.0.html, and Author Two, http://www.kboards.com/index.php/topic,188587.0.html. There is no evidence that Google Play drops author prices to free often. In fact, these are the only two incidents I've heard of. If Google Play is routinely dropping the price of other authors' books, those authors aren't talking about it.

Pre-Orders

Amazon, Smashwords, and D2D allow you to set up your book for pre-order. That means you can have a link for a book that isn't yet published. This is helpful if you're coordinating reviews or blog posts for the day the book is released. You don't have to wait until the night

---

[29] Google Play pricing guidelines, http://www.kboards.com/in-dex.php?topic=167655.0

before and do a soft launch (where you publish the book, but don't tell anybody until after the book is live on retail sites). When you set up a pre-order at Amazon, you have to upload a book file for the pre-order. Amazon uses that document to determine the estimated novel length for your book. So, if you upload a 10-page placeholder file for your pre-order, Amazon will list the book's length as 10 pages on the product page. Upload a file of roughly the right length, even if it isn't final, so you get product page information that's close to accurate. Pre-orders are not supposed to offer a Look Inside preview.

At Amazon and Smashwords, you have to have your pre-order final copy uploaded at least 10 days prior to the On Sale date. While D2D offers pre-orders, its website does not list the parameters for setting up a preorder.

Amazon penalizes authors who don't make their preorder deadlines. You can set up a preorder up to 90 days in advance of the On Sale date. However, your final manuscript must be uploaded 10 days prior to that On Sale date. If it isn't, Amazon will cancel your current pre-order, telling customers you are not publishing the book, and ban you from setting up pre-orders for one year. You're welcome to overestimate your On Sale date, as Amazon will allow you to move up the On Sale date if you want. It's just if you try to push it back that you get in trouble. You can find out more about setting up preorders on Amazon here: https://kdp.amazon.com/help?topicId=AGSSZQVFK ECO5.

While Amazon penalizes you if you miss your preorder date, readers will penalize you if you miss your Smashwords pre-order deadline. You see, Smashwords treats you like a big boy/girl, trusting you to do what you say. If you miss your deadline and have only uploaded a partial book, your pre-order buyers will receive just that partial book when your order goes live. Pre-orders are only available for Smashwords vendors (like Apple, Barnes and Noble, and Kobo); you cannot set up a pre-order for the Smashwords store. Some Smashwords vendors — Apple, for example — show a sample of the pre-order, so the file you upload to Smashwords should be as free from errors as you can make it (preferably edited). You can learn about pre-orders via Smashwords here: http://www.smashwords.com/preorder.

D2D has only four paragraphs of text explaining its pre-order process. The information doesn't say how much lead time the site needs, or file requirements, or whether buyers can preview the content. You can find the D2D info here: https://www.draft2digital.com/faq/#faq-category-preorders.

ISBNs & Other Book Identifiers

ISBN stands for International Standard Book Number. All print books need an ISBN. Generally, digital books don't need an ISBN. Only one company, Apple, requires digital books to have ISBNs.

While the ISBN is international, the standards for giving them out aren't. Therefore, I'll note that most countries provide ISBNs to authors for free. The United States is the exception. In the United States, authors must purchase ISBNs, and they are only sold via the company Bowker. At the writing of this book (2015), Bowker charged $125 for a single ISBN, $295 for a block of 10 ISBNs or $575 for a block of 100.

As ebooks don't require ISBNs, I wouldn't recommend U.S. authors purchase them. If you live stateside and go through a distributor, the distributor will provide you with a free ISBN you can use on your version of the ebook distributed through that company. If you live outside of the U.S., feel free to get an ISBN for your ebook, as it doesn't cost you anything.

ISBNs are used to identify a book and its edition. Therefore, you need an ISBN for each edition of your book. The digital version of your book will have a different ISBN from the paperback version, which will have a different ISBN from the hardback version. I recently gave a seminar on self-publishing, and there was a lot of confusion about ISBNs. Some people viewed the ISBN as a number that was the single identifier for a book (regardless of edition) to indicate that the book existed. Let's dispel that notion. ISBNs identify both the book AND the edition. If you create a second edition of your book (as professors often do), that new edition needs a new ISBN. That's a good thing, because then people can assure they're getting the most updated version of a book when they order based on ISBN. Most books are going to have multiple ISBNs, because they'll have multiple editions. In the U.S., the only way to get a single identifying number for your book is to get assigned a Library of Congress Catalog number[30]. Self-publishers are generally not eligible for these numbers because they are not given to the following class of books: ebooks, books paid for or

---

[30] Library of Congress Catalog Number info, http://www.loc.gov/publish/cip/faqs/

subsidized by the author, or books published by a company that publishes three or fewer authors.

Since you're going to need multiple ISBNs anyway, I don't see a downside to getting your ISBN free from a printer or distributor. Most print-on-demand firms like CreateSpace (we're discussing them in the next section) will give you a free ISBN for the print version of your book. Also, distributors Smashwords and D2D offer free ISBNs because they distribute to Apple, which requires the ebooks it sells to have an ISBN. The companies that offer free ISBNs do so because they sell authors' books, and they get paid a percentage every time a book is sold. If authors make no sales, these companies don't get paid. It behooves them to help authors make sales. One way they do that is by purchasing blocks of ISBNs cheap and assigning them to authors' books free so authors can publish. The one drawback of getting an ISBN from a company (either a print-on-demand firm or a distributor), is that it is merely assigned to you. You do not own it, so you cannot use that ISBN elsewhere. If you distribute through Smashwords, then decide to move to D2D, you can't take that Smashwords-assigned ISBN and use it at D2D. However, D2D will assign you a new one.

The reason most ebook stores do not require you to have an ISBN is because they assign you their own identifying number. Most notably, Amazon assigns a number called an ASIN. Most sites that advertise ebooks only ask for your Amazon ASIN. The ASIN number is assigned when you publish your book (or establish your pre-order), and you can find it on your KDP dashboard, as well as on the Amazon product page.

If you are in the U.S. and would like to purchase an ISBN for yourself, you may do so. I listed the prices earlier. If you are in a country that gives ISBNs free, then feel free to get ISBNs for all the editions of your book that you have. Your own ISBNs can be used for whatever place requests an ISBN. Therefore, your ebook edition, when published on Amazon, Barnes and Noble, Apple, and the Google Play store, will have the same ISBN number because it is your own.

If you live in the United States, please note that when you purchase an ISBN, you are declaring yourself a publisher. That's a lovely designation, however it may come with some unwanted obligations. Some local jurisdictions still think of publishers as those big businesses that print books, and as such, local laws may require "publishers" to obtain a publishing license and pay annual fees for operating a publishing business. If you choose to designate yourself a "publisher," check your local jurisdiction to find out if you are required to get licensed or pay any fees.

Creating Your Print Book

You've got your ebook all ready, and now you want a print book too. Or maybe you have no interest in an ebook and you just want to do print. (If that's the case, I do apologize for taking so long to get to print.)

Most self-publishers use a type of printing called print-on-demand (POD) to publish their books. In the old days, if you wanted to get paper books at a reasonable price, you had to order a large number from the printer (500+) and warehouse them at your house or some other location you controlled. Then you had to sell them by whatever means you could — from the trunk of your car; at arts festivals; online from your personal website, so you schlepped to the post office every time someone ordered a book. Well, POD eliminates all that. POD prints books one at a time. This means you don't have to warehouse books. Every time a customer orders, your printer prints that customer a single book and ships it to them. The single book cost is higher than if you ordered a large number of copies, but it is not an unreasonable price, $2.10 - $5 per copy, for a book of average length.

There are three POD companies that self-publishers tend to use: CreateSpace, Lulu, and Lightning Source's Ingram Spark.

Let's start with CreateSpace, which is owned by Amazon. CreateSpace has its own storefront, but also supplies books to Amazon.com and many of the other online book retailers (through a process called expanded distribution). Most indie authors use CreateSpace to produce paper copies of their book. The main reason is cost. Unless you're selling more than a 100 paper copies per month, it's cheaper to use CreateSpace to sell your books. There are no setup costs and you can, if you want, have your paperback for sale on Amazon, Barnes and Noble, and other retailers without spending a single penny.

To start, go to www.createspace.com and open a free account. After that, you will be able to upload your book to CreateSpace for printing. CreateSpace requires a PDF file for the interior of the book. You can create this file yourself, using their template (in Microsoft Word) as a guide. The MS Word template sets up all the formatting and allows you to paste your document into it. After you complete the MS Word document, simply save it as a PDF when you finish, and that document should work for your interior file.

You can also hire a formatter to create a formatted CreateSpace PDF for you. D2D offers a free CreateSpace conversion for your manuscript, but that converter was in beta mode at the time this book was written. The PDF looks nice as a PDF, however I have never attempted to upload this document to CreateSpace to see if it works. However you format your file, your CreateSpace interior must include your ISBN number (either one you own or your CreateSpace-assigned one).

When creating your paperback, you will need to pick the trim size of the book and whether you want white paper or cream colored paper. Cream colored paper costs more because it is slightly thicker, and requires a wider spine. The two most commonly used trim sizes, measured in inches, are the 6 x 9 and the 5.5 x 8.5. Either size is acceptable, but the 6x9 tends to be cheaper because its larger size uses fewer pages.

In addition to needing a formatted document file, you'll need a cover for your CreateSpace version of the book. Your cover should match the one on your ebook, so you'll need to upload a finished PDF of your book cover. As I mentioned in the cover section, you can buy a wraparound cover (one that includes the front, spine, and back) from your cover artist, or make it yourself. To get the dimensions your cover needs to be, go to http://www.createspace.com/Help/Book/Artwork.do, and enter the requested information for the book you're creating a cover for (trim size, page count, and paper type). Then you can download the appropriate cover template from CreateSpace. You can use the tutorial I created: http://rjcrayton.com/sp/tutorials. The tutorials are for those who purchased the book; please do not share.

Print Pricing

The last things you're going to pick from CreateSpace are the price of your book and whether you want expanded distribution, which allows your books to be sold at other retailers. If you pick expanded distribution, you will need to price your book higher because you earn less money in the expanded distribution payment plan. CreateSpace has a handy royalty calculator that will let you know how much profit you will get based on how much you charge, https://www.createspace.com/Products/Book/#content6:royaltyCalculator.

If you have both Amazon distribution and expanded distribution, and want to price your 250-page book at $9.99, you will earn $2.02 per book sold on Amazon, but only 2 cents on books sold via expanded distribution. Generally, people raise the price slightly so they can earn a little more on the expanded distribution. Raising the price to $10.99 would increase the Amazon royalty to $2.62 and the expanded distribution royalty to 42 cents. Why doesn't increasing the price a dollar increase your profit a dollar? It's due to the way books are sold to the places they're distributed. Amazon uses a basic wholesale pricing model where it expects to pay 50 percent of the list price for the book. So, if you sell your book for $10, Amazon is expected to pay $5 for it, and the difference between the $5 they pay for it and the $10 list price is Amazon's profit. When books are sold this way, this allows Amazon to discount the book's price and still earn a profit. So, your book's list price automatically has to be double your printing price (because the retailer only pays half the list price for the book). Your profit doesn't start until after you've doubled the printing price. CreateSpace also takes a cut of book sales when it distributes to other companies. It takes a smaller portion when it distributes through Amazon than when it distributes to the expanded channels. Authors always earn the least in the expanded distribution.

Printing costs for your book generally range from $2.15 to $5, depending on the length of your book. For example, my 260-page book, *Life First*, costs $3.97 to print, while my short story collection, *Four Mothers*, 86 pages, costs $2.15 to print. My longest book, *Second Life*, 288 pages, costs $4.30 to print. If you write fantasy, which can easily run 400-500 pages, you'll have much higher printing costs, and the minimum price for your paperback is going to be higher than the minimum price for someone who writes thriller or romance. Price your paperback book in a way that is both profitable and commiserate (or slightly lower) in price with other books in its genre. Look at book list prices, not the prices Amazon offers, which are often discounted, as Amazon pays the wholesale price and gives customers a discount by reducing its profit. So, if books in your genre list for $16, and you can make a profit at $12, make your list price somewhere between $12 and $16. Don't make your list price $17.99 if no other books in that category are selling that high.

Matching Your Print with Your Ebook

If you have both an ebook and print version of the same book, you'll need to make sure they're matched up. The easiest way to do this is to make sure the books have the exact same title done the same way. Why wouldn't your book have the exact same title? This most commonly happens when you have subtitles. For my book, *Third Life: Taken*, I had to manually link the paperback and ebook versions, because when I input the name on CreateSpace, I just used Third Life (more for shorthand for myself). However, the title you enter when you set up the book isn't just shorthand. It's what goes to Amazon and the other distributors (if you pick expanded distribution). In order to change the title after you've created it, you must email CreateSpace customer service. If, for some reason, your books still don't get linked, you can link them manually on Amazon.com by going to Amazon's Author Central and selecting your book. (Check the *Marketing* section, p. 87, for information on Author Central.) If you are selling your print book through CreateSpace's expanded distribution (which goes to BarnesandNoble.com and other online stores), your print book won't link up with the ebook version at Barnes and Noble if the titles aren't exactly the same. For people whose ebooks aren't exclusive to Amazon, it's important to make sure that title is correct.

Most self-published authors create their ebook version first and their print version second. There are a couple of reasons for this. First, most self-publishers earn the bulk of their income from ebook sales, so there is no rush to finish the print version. The second is that they sometimes like to have the books on the market a few weeks to see if readers report any formatting problems or typos. Even with an editor, things can get missed, and some people prefer to let things shake out prior to fixing their book in a more permanent form (print). People also wait on print because they have to format the book. The formatting is different enough that, if you're in a hurry to get the book out, it's easier to simply postpone the print edition.

Proofing. After your book has been approved by CreateSpace, you can order a proof copy. The proof will cost the price of printing, along with shipping cost. So, perhaps $4 for the book and $4 to ship it. When you receive your proof copy, you should review it and look for both formatting errors and any typos you might have missed. I know some people like to do their ebook proofing by printing a CreateSpace proof copy to review. If you truly don't wish to spend any money, you can review a digital proof that you can download. However, I recommend having the printed copy of the proof come to you. Proofs generally ship within a day or two of ordering. Once a book has been approved for sale, and you order a copy, those books print and ship slower.

A quick note. CreateSpace has an option to convert your print book to an ebook. I know at least one writer who tried this and said the conversion turned out horrible. So, if you happen to get your print book done first and are considering using this conversion, don't assume it will look great. You can try it, but don't approve that version to Amazon unless you've tested it and are happy with the way it looks.

Pre-Orders. There is no easy way to do pre-orders for print books. Not on CreateSpace, Lightning Source, or Lulu. However, if you would like to set up an account at Amazon Advantage, there is a complicated way to do this. It's not something I've done because I don't sell enough print copies for it be worth my time to do. The method is described on the CreateSpace Community Forum: https://www.create space.com/en/community/thread/21239. To use the method, you must start it prior to publishing your book on CreateSpace, so read the instructions before you get too deep into uploading your book.

Lightning Source & Lulu

Most people use CreateSpace because they can get the paperback setup at no cost to themselves, and because it works so well with Amazon. However, CreateSpace only offers paperbacks. If you'd like a hardback copy of your book — and some people do — you have to go elsewhere. Also, if you start selling a lot of paperback copies of your books, you might want to switch to Lightning Source's Ingram Spark, which offers cheaper publishing prices per book but has a setup fee.

So, let's start with the hardback issue. Both Lightning Source and Lulu allow authors to create hardback versions of their books. If you just want one or two copies, go with Lulu, as they do the hardbacks POD. It will be slightly expensive, but definitely worth the expense if hardcover is your thing. Some people say books of photography are done better by Lulu as well. Like CreateSpace, it's free to setup your books at Lulu. Proofs and printed books tend to be a little more expensive per unit than CreateSpace.

Lightning Source (under its Ingram Spark imprint) is a POD company, but it has more experience working with small publishers, rather than individual authors who are self-publishing. The company has a reputation for doing a good job, but they use a more traditional model. They charge a setup fee for each book you want to print. At press time, that fee was $49. Overall, the per-book prices for printing, after the setup fee is paid, are cheaper than CreateSpace's. However, most self-publishers don't sell enough paperback copies of their book to make up for the setup fee. If you find that you are selling a lot of paperback books, you may want to switch to Lightning Source, as, over the course of hundreds or thousands of books, the difference in pricing will cut into your profit. You would not want to use Lightning Source only to get a handful of copies of your book, as you will not offset the setup fee.

Getting Paid

How you get paid for your work depends on the vendor. Amazon pays monthly with a 60-day delay. So, you'll get paid two months after the month ends. Sales made in September won't be paid until December. Amazon used to have a minimum payment requirement (where you had to earn a minimum of $10 to be paid). However, Amazon jettisoned this requirement. If you have one sale of a 99 cent book that netted you a 35 cent payment, you'll get a 35 cent payment from Amazon. Before you say, "Gee, I really hope I don't have a 35 cent month," you probably will. Not because you don't sell lots of books on Amazon.com, but because most people sell fewer books on the international Amazons. International Amazons? Yes. Amazon.com doesn't sell books in England. Amazon.co.uk sells books in England. Many countries have their own Amazon sites (Canada, Australia, Germany, and Japan). When you sign up to sell your books, you can pick which countries to sell in. I suggest picking them all. But, that also means you'll get income that's not just from Amazon.com sales. I've gotten itty bitty payments before, and it's because I sold a single book in Germany or some country that isn't in the Amazon.com accounting.

Many vendors pay similar to Amazon — monthly with a 60-day delay — while some pay quarterly. Unlike Amazon, most retailers have a minimum payment requirement. Generally the requirement is $10 in royalties if you want it paid to an electronic account. If you want a paper check, most companies will mail it to you, but they have a larger minimum ($25 - $100) and may charge you a processing fee (one company charges $8 to process a check). If you're not selling a lot on those sites, you won't see money from them until your sales surpass the minimum to get paid.

The print vendors pay similarly. CreateSpace pays book royalties "at the end of the following month. For example, you will receive your royalty payment at the end of March for the sales you made in February." Lulu and Lightning Source's Ingram Spark pay similarly, but will take longer to get data about book sales, because they have to wait 6-8 weeks to get the data from their vendors. CreateSpace, because it's owned by Amazon, gets information about Amazon sales fairly quickly, but takes just as long as Lulu and Lightning Source's Ingram Spark to get sales info from outside vendors. Below, I've pasted the payment schedule information for all the digital and print sites I've listed in the book:

Amazon: https://kdp.amazon.com/help?topicId=AE24XS35AM53P

NookPress: http://cp-barnesandnoble.kb.net/kb/?ArticleId=4378&source=Article&c=12&cid=28

Smashwords: https://www.smashwords.com/about/supportfaq#Royalties

Draft2Digital: https://www.draft2digital.com/faq/#faq-category-payment

AllRomance Ebooks: http://www.allromanceebooks.com/termsOfAgreement.html

Google Play: https://support.google.com/books/partner/answer/6009580?hl=en

Libiro: http://www.libiro.com/index.php?route=information/information&information_id=6

CreateSpace: https://www.createspace.com/Help/Rights/Policies.jsp#payments

Lulu: http://www.lulu.com/blog/2011/08/when-do-i-get-paid-how-to-check-your-creator-revenue/

Lightning Source's Ingram Spark: https://www.ingramspark.com/Portal/FAQ#How and when am I paid for my sales?

Getting Into Bookstores and Libraries

While it's easy to get into online stores, it's not as easy to get into physical places, but it can be done. So, let's talk about how to get your books into bookstores and libraries.

Bookstores. The reality is most self-published books don't make it to bookstore shelves. Physical stores, unlike online stores, are limited by space. They don't have an unlimited amount of space and the shelves they do have are in high demand. Each year, according to Bowker, the traditional publishing industry publishes 300,000 books. Those publishers have people whose job it is to make sure they get their books in bookstores across the nation. Self-publishers, who add another 2 million books to the market annually, can't compete on a national level. However, you can get your book into local bookstores.

To do so, research the local bookstore options to see what stores are in your area. Local, independent stores may be keener to accept an indie author than a chain store, such as a Barnes and Noble or Books-a-Million. Always research the store you want to get into. Check out its website and mentions on local writing websites. The store may be indie friendly and have a set method for indies who want to have their book in the store. If you can't find any guidelines online, call the store and find out the process. Then set up a meeting with the manager (or the appropriate acquisitions person) for five or ten minutes to talk about stocking your book at the store or a possible author event, such as a book signing. You want to call first, rather than just stopping by, as the person you need to convince might not be there or might be busy when you happen to stop in. At your meeting, you want to discuss any high points about your book. Has it won any awards? Is it going to be a book club selection for a local group who might come to this store to purchase copies? Does it have stellar reviews or endorsements? You also want to leave a copy of the book with the decision maker so he or she can read through it. The worst thing that can happen is the bookstore says no. If so, move on and try someplace else.

While a bookstore is the ideal place for a book, there are other stores that are suited to carrying books. If there is a local tie-in, there may be a store that wants to carry it. If you're in Vermont and you have a book of pancake recipes, maybe a local syrup shop would carry your book. If the book is a cozy mystery set in a bed and breakfast, perhaps the local B&B would carry a few copies. Feel free to think outside the box, if you'd like to see your book sold in local venues. For example, in the Washington, DC-area, there is a restaurant chain called Busboys and Poets (a reference to Langston Hughes' turn as a busboy to pay the bills while he tried to build his writing career). It has a bookstore that carries independent books and a procedure local authors can use if they wish to be in the bookstore. If you have any store like that in your area, it's a place you may want to try to get into.

Libraries. Local libraries like to have local authors, and they often have a program to evaluate the inclusion of local authors in the collection. To find out how your library system (either county or city) acquires local author books, start by checking its website. Some library systems post their guidelines. If the library doesn't post guidelines, call the branch and find out if they have a way for local authors to submit their books for review. Submit your book via the guidelines the library provides.

Another way to get into libraries is through fans. All library systems have a way for patrons to suggest books for purchase. If your fans suggest your book, the library system may purchase a copy. Library requirements for patron-suggested purchases differ depending on the library system. Back in the late 90s, when I covered the Kansas City Public libraries for the *Kansas City Star*, the policy was that if three customers requested a book, the library system would purchase the book. At my own library system, I submitted an online customer comment noting that I was surprised the library didn't have a copy of a book I'd seen listed on a year-end list of "Best Books for Women to Read in 2012." It was more intended to be an informational email, but two weeks later, I got an email saying the book was on hold for me. The library system had ordered it. So, if you want your books in libraries, reader requests are often the way to go.

Updating Your Book

Let's say you've gotten your ebook published and you think it's great. But then a friend emails you and tells you they've found some typos. How do you fix that? This is why I suggested doing the formatting yourself in Microsoft Word rather than hiring a formatter. If you used a Word file, you can simply make the changes, then go and re-upload the document to whichever retailers you published at. This is also why I mentioned file naming conventions earlier. Your corrected file should have the new date in its name so you know this is the most recent version — the one where you corrected the typos your friend was kind enough to point out. To have your corrected version replace the old version, you have to "republish" the book. I put that in quotes, because for most vendors to make a change to the book, you have to make the changes you want, and then click "Publish." In essence, you are republishing the book. The original publication date should stay the same when you do this, but the updated file version will be available for any new purchasers. For people who previously purchased the book, some vendors have a way for the reader to get file updates. However, most readers don't update files of a book they've already read. If a reader purchased your book, but never sent it to their device (which can happen), then they'll download the most recent copy of your book when they do get around to sending it to their device. However, if they purchased it and did send it to their device, but didn't start reading it, then they'll read the old version — unless they actively decide to see if there's a new version of the book. Kindle users can check book versions on the Manage Your Content and Devices section of Amazon's website.

To update your CreateSpace print files, you have to go click on your book (on your Member Dashboard), then click on Interior. When taken to the upload screen, add the new PDF file you wish to use. When you change the interior file, CreateSpace still goes through the cover review process, so you'll have to wait the 24 hours for them to finish that review before you can make your book live. I don't recommend ordering a paper proof for updates. Generally, if your PDF proof copy looks fairly similar to the last paper proof you received (except it's fixed the typos your friend pointed out), then it's fine to just approve it. I have never used Lulu or Lightning Source for print distribution, but based on their online Q&As, the change process seems to be similar.

Unpublishing

You may want to remove your book from sale. All vendors have an option for doing this. It is generally called "unpublish." Most people like having their books for sale, but sometimes there are good reasons to unpublish. If you had distributed your books to all vendors and now you want to join KDP Select, you'll need to pull your book from all the other vendors. If you wrote a how-to book and it's full of old information, perhaps you want to unpublish it, rather than simply updating the book. Some people choose to switch distributors. The books originally published through distributor one have to be unpublished before they can be switched over to distributor two. If you unpublish your book, it might lose all the reviews it garnered at the site, so be sure you really don't want it published any longer. The loss of reviews is less of a factor if you truly don't want the book out there, rather than if you're unpublishing it simply so you can switch distributors or try KDP Select. In those instances, that same book is likely going to be on the market again and you'd like to have those reviews. If you'd like to improve your chances of keeping your reviews, I suggest you offer a paperback copy of your book through expanded distribution on CreateSpace. I had a book that was in KDP Select and never getting borrowed. I decided to move the book to wider distribution. The day the book appeared on Barnes and Noble's site, I noticed it had a review. "Yay," I thought. "I sold a copy already AND the person left a review!" Then I realized the review was from four months earlier. I was baffled, until, until I realized the review had been posted to the print version of the book. Barnes and Noble had merged the ebook and print book, so when viewers saw the book's product page, they had the option of buying the print version or the ebook version. Because of this, the earlier review was showing. If you also have a print version of your book, your reviews are more likely to survive a distributor switch, because the reviews should stick to the print version of the book, even though you unpublish your ebook. This isn't guaranteed, but it's the best shot you have at getting them to stick. If you simply have an ebook and unpublish it, the reviews will likely disappear with it forever.

Step 4 Checklist

Front Matter

_____ Copyright Page

_____ Title Page

_____ Dedication

_____ Active TOC

_____ Review Quotes*

_____ Subscribe Request*

Back Matter

_____ Book Preview

_____ Leave a Review

_____ Acknowledgements*

_____ About the Author

_____ Also by Author

_____ Subscribe Request*

_____ Review Quotes*

_____ Book Club Questions

Formatted Book For:

_____Smashwords

_____Draft2Digital

_____Amazon

_____Apple iTunes^

_____NookPress

_____CreateSpace

_____Google Play^

_____All Romance ebooks^

_____Libiro^

^ You cannot submit Microsoft Word files to these companies. You will need a formatted epub (or possibly PDF) document.

Pre-Publish Items

_____ BISAC categories selected

_____ Keywords selected

_____ Price selected

_____ Reviewed book preview

_____ ISBN for print

_____ Email account created

_____ Bank account established

_____ Registered Copyright

Published To:

_____ Amazon

_____ Google Play

_____ Libiro

_____ All Romance ebooks

_____ Kobo

_____ Barnes and Noble

_____ Apple

Smashwords

_____ Smashwords Store

_____ Kobo

_____ Barnes and Noble

_____ Apple

_____ Oyster

_____ ScribD

_____ OverDrive

_____ Page Foundry

_____ FlipKart

_____ Library Direct

_____ Baker & Taylor

Draft2Digital

_____ Kobo

_____ Barnes and Noble

_____ Apple

Print

CreateSpace

_____ Amazon

_____ Expanded Distribution

_____ Lulu

_____ Lightning Source's Ingram Spark

STEP 5: MARKETING

Your book is out there and available to the public now. How do you market it? In this section, we'll talk about the most essential things you'll need in your arsenal to get your book (or books) selling. The most basic things you need in your author marketing arsenal include a website, Goodreads page, and Amazon Author page. Next you'll need reviews and advertising — two important strategies for any authors who want to earn money. After that we'll talk about various strategies people use to get their books exposed to readers, including making books free, mailing lists, blogs, social media, and a couple of other ideas. All marketing techniques discussed, unless they specifically state you need to have a finished book as part of them, can be done prior to publishing your books. Let's get started.

Website

Every author needs a website. When fans Google you, the first hit should be your author website.

Are websites hard to create or expensive? Nope. For most first-time authors, I'd recommend setting up a website via WordPress or Blogspot.com. Both are free to set up, and allow you to include a static web page, as well as a blog. Neither requires active knowledge of html (hypertext markup language), the programming language used for websites. Both are WYSIWYG (What you see is what you get).

You should set up your author website before your book is published. That way, it's all ready when you publish. Also, having it set up before hand, allows you to do some pre-publication publicity. If you guest blog or have an interview prior to the book's publication, people who hear about you or see you have some place to go.

When people visit your web site, there are three sections they absolutely expect you to have: an About section that tells about you as an author and includes your author bio and a professional looking author photo (do-it-yourself professional photo tips here: http://www.indies unlimited.com/2014/01/14/author-portraits-a-how-to/); a Books section, which lists your books and where to purchase them; and a Contact section, which provides a contact form for fans to email you. For those using a pseudonym, you don't have to include an author picture. Some authors with pseudonyms choose to use a favorite static shot, like a nature shot or one of the book covers in place of the author photo. The bio for a pseudonym doesn't have to be long. It can give a little pertinent information about your pseudonym personality. For example, if all your writing is done under an erotic pseudonym, then this might be what your pseudonym bio looks like: "Trixie Leggz writes erotica, specializing in BDSM and BWWM stories. The first novel in her Chained series, *Up Against the Wall*, was published in January 2015 and three more titles are forthcoming." If you're writing under multiple names, see the section called Marketing Additional Pseudonyms.

In addition to the must-have sections, you can have the following sections: Subscribe, where readers can subscribe your mailing list; Press, where you can include news articles, interviews and a Press Kit; Blog, where you host your blog (we talk blogs later in this section); and Extras, a place where readers can find content that supplements your books, such as deleted scenes or additional character background information.

For those unfamiliar with the term, a press kit was traditionally a folder handed to reporters that included all the background information they need to write a story on an individual. It included high resolution photos that could be printed in newspapers or magazines, an author bio, and a book sheet that included some excerpts from the book and perhaps review quotes. In the online world, it's good enough to say Press Kit on a page and put links to these things beneath that. You want to link to high-resolution author photos and high resolution book covers. Most photos used on the web are not high resolution. They are small in size 100-200 kb, which look fine. For print, people want high-res (1mb+) images. Here are some tips for creating an online press kit: http://www.indiesunlimited.com/2012/08/28/how-to-build-a-press-room-on-your-website/.

Both WordPress and Blogspot.com let you purchase a personal domain name (like www.myname.com) to use as a front for their backbone site, so no one will know you're not a programming whiz. WordPress is the most popular website hosts, and there are all sorts of plugins that are free and supplement the basic WordPress site. These plugins allow your site to look cool and do tricky html without you having to program it yourself. With WordPress, if you want to get your own host (rather than using wordpress.com), that's easy to do. WordPress does have some restrictions on selling products and certain types of advertisements on WordPress-hosted sites. So, read the terms of service carefully. BlogSpot.com has fewer restrictions, and some authors go with them because of this.

Whichever place pick, make sure your site looks professional. If you'd like to know what some successful indie authors' websites look like, try:

http://jakonrath.com/
http://www.sexyawesomebooks.com/#!/HOME
http://www.hughhowey.com/
http://www.agriddle.com/
http://www.jfpenn.com/

These are all professional sites with varying degrees of fanciness. If there is a particular one you wish to emulate, you can see if the site gives credit to a designer. If it does, you can contact that designer. If that designer is out of your price range, talk to a web person who is in your price range (such as a friend who will do it for free), and show them the site. They may be able to emulate it for you, so long as they have a blueprint of what you want.

If you're starting out self-publishing, don't waste money on building an elaborate website. Your book will sell books, not your website. If you've got limited money, it's the content that will sell books and that's where most of your money should be spent.

Goodreads & Amazon Author Pages

In addition to setting up a website, you should also set up two other author pages: Amazon and Goodreads.

Goodreads. After you've set up your website, you should set up your Goodreads Author Page. Goodreads is a site for readers, and hardcore readers love it. They flock there to discuss books and learn about new books they should read. If you're an author, you want to be there. Goodreads is great for readers because it helps them keep track of their books. If they read some books from the library, some from Amazon and some from iTunes, Goodreads is the one place they can go to input all the data. You'll catch lots of readers there.

Like your website, you can create a Goodreads Author Page before your book comes out. Because Goodreads is a reader-based site, you'll need to join the site as a reader. Once you've joined as a reader, you need to create a page for your book. You add a book to Goodreads using this page: https://www.goodreads.com/book/new (you need to be logged in for this page to work). In the publication date field, include the date in the future that your book will be published. You'll need the standard book info, including title, author, cover image, and description. It has fields for your ISBN or ASIN, but pre-publication you won't have that. Just be sure to update the page once you publish the book. After your book page is up, you need to claim your book, saying you are the author.

When you claim your book, you can apply for an author account (see the FAQ here: https://www.goodreads.com/author/program). You must have a book in the Goodreads database before you can get an author account. If you waited until after your book was published to create an author account, it's possible a zealous Goodreads user stumbled across your book, read it, and added it to the database. More likely is that you will have to add your book to the database and then claim it. Please be advised that if you have a pseudonym, you will need to create a Goodreads account in the name of that pseudonym to claim any books written by that pseudonym.

Once you've been approved for an author account, you'll need to set up your Goodreads author page. Much like your website About page, the Goodreads Author Page should include an author photo and an author bio. Again, if you are writing under a pseudonym and don't want to reveal your identity, you can skip the picture. You are also able to link your blog to your author page so readers can see your most recent blog posts. Goodreads offers an author Q&A section and provides some initial questions for you to answer. Feel free to answer these if you have time. It will make your Goodreads Author page a little more robust.

Amazon readers tend to find author information via Amazon's author pages. Other sites, such as Apple, Kobo and Barnes and Noble, don't have author pages. When readers from those sites want to look up an author, they often turn to Goodreads.

Amazon. This seems like a good segue into Amazon's author pages. Amazon's Author Central allows you to create your Amazon Author Page. Whenever a book page appears on Amazon, the author's name is listed beneath the title. Generally, when you click the hyperlinked name, it will take you to the Amazon Author Page, which lists the author's bio, all the books the author has published on Amazon, and has the option to include videos, Twitter and blog feeds (we'll talk about Twitter and blogs in the Social Media section).

It's important to create an Amazon Author Page, so readers can quickly access your other books. If the reader enjoyed one of your books and is now looking for something else by you to read, they'll click your name and be able to see all your others books. Also, it's possible the reader is slightly intrigued by your book's cover, but not enough to buy it. They might be curious if you have other interesting books and check out your author page. If they see a cover they like even more, they could end up buying that book. Given that buyers often make snap, split-second decisions on book purchases, it's key to give them as many opportunities as possible to drill down and get more information.

To get an Amazon Author page, you need to create an account at https://authorcentral.amazon.com. You can only set up an Amazon Author Page after your book is published (either as a regular publication or pre-order). You can use the same username and password as you use for your KDP account. You just need to set up the account separately. Once your account is set up, you need to go and claim your books. You'll type in your author name and Author Central will give you a list of books. Just click your books to claim them. If you write under a pseudonym, Author Central will say, "Hey, that name doesn't match yours," and ask if it's a pseudonym. You will say yes, and Author Central will direct you to set up a pseudonym profile. You can manage up to three pseudonyms from one Author Central account. If you use more than one author name, you will get a drop-down menu that allows you to toggle between personalities. All your pseudonyms can get their own author pages. Because you can only have three names per Author Central account, you will need to set up a second Author Central account if you need more pseudonyms. All of your published books, no matter how many pseudonyms, should be published under one KDP account. Only Author Central requires you to create more accounts if you have multiple pseudonyms. Most writers generally don't have a need for more than three pseudonyms. However, it's not uncommon for erotica writers to use multiple pseudonyms.

Amazon sells worldwide; unfortunately it uses a different domain name for many countries it sells in. Books sold in the United Kingdom are sold via http://amazon.co.uk. Amazon has chosen to tie its author pages with each individual country-particular Amazon site. Therefore, if you use the link I provided above, your Amazon Author Page will only be available to Amazon.com users. If you want your Amazon UK readers to see your bio, you have to set up an Author Central account for their county. There are four additional Author Centrals. You can set up pages on each site via these links (the text may be in a different language, but the placement is similar enough that you should be able to figure out where things go):

France: https://authorcentral.amazon.fr
UK: https://authorcentral.amazon.co.uk/gp/landing
Germany: https://authorcentral.amazon.de/gp/landing
Japan: https://authorcentral.amazon.co.jp/gp/landing

At press time, the Canadian and Australian Amazon sites did not have their own Author Central pages. Users in those countries just won't get to see your author page.

Reviews

You've got a website and author pages, so you're on your way. Now you need to focus on the specific book you're publishing, and that means getting reviews. Ever go to Amazon and see a book with no reviews? What's the first thing that crosses your mind when that happens? Probably that the book is untested and might not be very good.

Well, that's what readers will think when they see your book has no reviews. That means you need reviews. How do you get them? Start with your beta readers. They've read the book and have an idea whether they liked it or not. When your book comes out, tell your beta readers the book is available and ask them to leave a review. Tell them you'd be glad to provide an electronic copy of the final book, if they'd like (some people don't want to leave a review for the book without seeing the final version, particularly if the earlier version had an excessive number of typos or problems). It's good to get beta reader reviews because they can leave a review fairly soon after the book is published, often much quicker than the amount of time it would take for a person to buy and read the book from scratch.

Beyond your betas, where do you look? Readers. You'll want to let your readers know that you want reviews. If you followed the advice on back matter, you should have requested readers leave a review on the website they purchased the book, as well as on the Goodreads page for the book. This may turn up some reviews for your book, depending on how widely read your book is. While I couldn't find statistics on how often readers leave reviews, the prevailing wisdom is that you have to sell a fair number of books to get reviews. For new books with few sales, this plea in the back may not reach enough readers to bring a lot of reviews. However, you still want it there, in case it inspires a reader to leave a review.

Another way to garner reviews is through the newsletter you send to your mailing list (and we'll talk in more detail about mailing lists shortly). In those mailings, it's fine to ask readers to leave a review if they enjoyed the book.

If people who've bought your book aren't leaving reviews, then you can offer to give people a free copy of your book in exchange for a review. Sites like Goodreads and LibraryThing (a social site for readers similar to Goodreads) offer what's commonly referred to as R4R (Read for Review) programs. If you use these programs, you can send the reader a copy of your book in exchange for an honest review. All the Goodreads R4R programs I've seen have a review deadline — usually 3 to 4 weeks after the reader is sent the book.

R4R programs are a little hit-and-miss. First off, I've seen many discussion boards warning authors not to use Goodreads reviewers because they're too harsh. I can't say whether readers on Goodreads are harsher than others, but they certainly take the "give an honest review" thing seriously, so be prepared for honest opinions, whether they be good or bad. Goodreads users tend to be hardcore readers, so they may like a book a lot and still give it just 3 stars because it didn't dazzle them. This may be where some of the complaints of "harsh" reviews come from.

The other issue with R4R is, sometimes the people who join R4R groups are unreliable. They don't leave a review after receiving the book. It happens, but you should definitely not harass the reader who did so. It's part of the R4R life, and if it's unacceptable to you, don't do read for review. Antagonizing a reader who didn't review your book is most likely to land you with a nasty one-star review or worse (a reader who blogs regularly and writes a post claiming you harassed him because his mother died and he didn't get a chance to leave a review in timely fashion).

If you're getting a lackluster response from those who promised to review your book, you can send an email to all the people who received a book but haven't left a review yet. Say something like, "Just wanted to make sure everyone had the links for where to leave reviews for BOOKNAME. Thanks so much for agreeing to read and review my book!" Of course, include the links to your book pages in the email. All Goodreads groups have a moderator, and R4R programs generally have a person in charge as a liaison. If you get a really low return rate (10 people receive your book and only 1 person leaves a review), you can ask the moderator to remind reviewers to complete the review. Beyond those types of gentle nudges, there's not a whole lot more you can do with readers who don't leave a review. Being mean, nasty and demanding will backfire on you. If it's not working out the way you wanted, it's best to just let it go and chalk it up to a "lesson-learned" experience.

In addition to R4R programs on reader sites, there are many blogs that review books. These review bloggers are folks who leave honest reviews and tend to post on their review blog as well as Amazon, Goodreads and other sites where books are sold. That's a good thing. These reviewers have a broad reach, as their blog, presumably, has at least a few followers or regular readers. Many blogs publicize their number of followers and subscribers. A site with big numbers is a good opportunity to reach many readers. Still, submit to review blogs that have only a few (or an indeterminate number of) subscribers, because they're likely to still leave a review on Amazon. Also, their review will likely get picked up by the Google search algorithms, and when people search your book title, that blog post will be one of several hits that shows up.

The key thing to remember with all reviews, whether by review blogs, Goodreads users or regular buyers, is that they're not always good. The reviewer may hate your book, or they may love it, or they may think it's ho hum. While you can do whatever you want in private, don't get publicly upset if a reviewer gives your book a bad review. It happens. If the reviewer gives a scathing review for things you can change (like it's full of grammatical errors), just be thankful someone gave you an honest opinion and try to correct it. If the reviewer just hates the book, then accept that, as you're not going to change the person's mind. I'm sure there's been a very popular book out there that you didn't love. Not everyone is going to love every book. If the reviewer likes your book, then jump for joy. If the reviewer hates it, move on.

Where do you find review blogs? There are a bunch, but I'll list a couple right here:

Big Al's Books and Pals
http://booksandpals.blogspot.com/p/submitting-book-for-review.html

BestChicklit.com
http://bestchicklit.com/?page_id=2044

Rabid Readers
http://www.rabidreaders.com/about-us/

Chuckles Book Cave
http://chucklesbookcave.blogspot.co.uk/

An aggregate list of review sites at The IndieView
http://www.theindieview.com/indie-reviewers/

An aggregate list of review sites at Indie Book Reviewer
https://indiebookreviewer.wordpress.com/

Anytime you want your book reviewed by a blog, be sure to read and follow the submission guidelines (above, I tried to link to the submission pages, if possible). These blogs get way more submissions than they have time to read, so the best way to maximize your chances of getting selected for review is to follow the submission instructions. If the blog wants you to swear that you did 10 push-ups prior to sending the email, then do 10 push-ups, swear to it and send the email. No sites have onerous requirements such as those, but some want you to send the book and they'll review it if they get a chance, while others want you to send a query first and only send your book if you get a positive response. Indies Unlimited had a post that asked book bloggers what got them to pick a book for review. The answers[31] may be useful to you in crafting the email you send to reviewers.

The more books you get into readers' hands (either through sales or freebies), the more likely you are to get reviews. Getting your book out there and read is the only way you'll get reviews. In addition to requesting reviews after the book is out, you can also request a review before your book is published. You send out an ARC (Advanced Review Copy) of your book to any reviewer who has agreed to review your book in advance. ARC requests need to go out at least 6 weeks prior to the book's publication to make sure the reviewer has time to complete the review for release date. You'll send ARC requests the same way you send out other review requests. Follow guidelines and offer up a tantalizing blurb. You can send an electronic or paper version of the ARC. It is acceptable to send out an ARC that hasn't had a final edit. On the first page of your ARC, put the words: "This is an UNCORRECTED PROOF. It may contain errors that will not be in the final, published version. This copy is intended for content review. Do not share with others." The key is that ARC readers know it may contain errors. If you're sending an unedited ARC, please do your best to get the manuscript as clean as possible.

Some authors are concerned about the idea of sending electronic files around to reviewers, who could copy them and pass them on to others or upload them to file sharing sites. While those things could happen, they are highly unlikely to occur. I have never heard of a reviewer even being accused of such a thing. Most reviewers are pretty up front. You are in the driver's seat with reviews you request, so only reach out to people you feel comfortable with. If a person you're not comfortable with, unsolicited, requests a review copy, you can politely

---

[31] What reviewers want article, http://indiesunlimited.com/2015/03/10/what-do-book-reviewers-really-really-want/

decline, telling them that you've run out of the allotted copies for review. Due to concerns about viruses, some reviewers will want a coupon code to download the book from a legitimate site, such as Smashwords, rather than receiving an emailed file.

Lastly, let me note that there are many sites that charge for reviews, including Kirkus, which is a big name in the review business. Some libraries use Kirkus reviews in evaluating books for inclusion in their library system. Unfortunately, Kirkus charges to review self-published books (even though it reviews traditionally published works for free). I don't recommend paying for reviews. It feels smarmy, and you're really better off just offering a book free in return for a review.

These companies that charge for reviews are making money off of someone, so clearly people are doing it. Remember that even if you pay for the review, they're not guaranteeing it will be positive. Many people have posted they've paid several hundred dollars for a Kirkus review to get something lackluster or scathing. You can get lackluster and scathing for free, so why pay? If you do choose to pay for a review, please note that the reviewer cannot leave that review on your Amazon book page. It is against Amazon's terms of service to include paid reviews in the customer review area. You can only use quotes from paid reviews in the area that says, "Editorial Reviews." Generally, paid reviews can only be used in promotional material, as many consumer sites have policies that prohibit paid reviews from being left in the "customer review" fields.

Discount Advertising Sites

Once your book has some reviews, you can start advertising it. Most indie authors advertise their books on discount advertising sites. These sites can introduce your book to a slew of new readers, but they require discounting your book, usually. Also, many of these sites have a minimum number of reviews your book must have before they will accept it for advertising. Minimums range from 4 reviews on smaller sites to as many as 25 on the big name sites.

Let's start with the crème de la crème of the advertising sites: Book-Bub (http://www.bookbub.com). This site is incredibly hard to get accepted to and incredibly expensive, once you get accepted. However, it tends to be worth the money, based on reports. There's not a person I've spoken to who's done a BookBub and gotten fewer than 1,300 sales for a 99 cent priced ebook. That boost in sales will move your book up the Amazon ranking chart, probably to the top of its category. When a book is in the top of its category (such as dystopia, or historical romance), it will also get some browsers who see it's a top-ranked book and buy it on impulse. We talked about category rankings earlier, but just a quick reminder: each subcategory, such as medical thriller, has its own bestseller list. The number of books it takes you become the number one bestseller in a subcategory is going to be less than the number of books it takes you to be ranked the number one bestseller in an overall category. For example, Mystery & Thrillers is an overall category. To be the number one selling book in that category, you have to sell better than all the other mystery and thriller books on Amazon. That's a lot of books. However, if you are listed in the medical thrillers subcategory, you would have to sell a lot fewer books to be the number one best seller on the medical thrillers list. To be number one in Mystery and Thriller, you might need to sell 500 books in a single day. To be number one in Medical Thrillers, you might only need to sell 70 books in a given day. That is why it is really important to get categorized properly. If you are No. 1 on the Medical Thrillers list, buyers in that genre will see you and might take a chance. However, if you're number 99 on the Mystery & Thrillers list, you're unlikely to be seen by very many.

If an ebook does really well, it could get high ranking in Amazon's overall store, too. However, I wouldn't expect that with most advertisers, as you need to sell upwards of 3,000 ebooks in a day to reach the top spot in Amazon's overall ranking (i.e. the top selling book in all of Amazon, in any category). A quick note: ebook and paperback sales rank are done separately, so the number one ebook may be different than the number one paperback sale.

If you are lucky enough to get a BookBub — and they reject 90 percent of the applicants — schedule some other advertisements in advance of it. The reason is this: Amazon prefers your book to have a slow and steady build, and its algorithms reward books that have one or two sales, then three sales the next day, then 10 sales, then maybe 20. They "reward" books by suggesting them to other Amazon readers (at no cost to you).

If you get a big burst of sales then taper off, Amazon algorithms do nothing to promote you (the emails customers get in their inboxes suggesting books). However, if you have a slow build, the algorithms assume it's more natural, that your book is catching on with readers and will reward you in the algorithms. What are the algorithms? Well, those are the if-then programming scenarios that are the underpinnings of how Amazon works. For example, if a book sells 20 copies a day for ten days in a row, Amazon would then email readers who have bought a book in that category in the past week and suggest they buy the book that is selling 20 copies a day. However that is just an example of how the algorithms might work. No one knows what the algorithms actually say because Amazon won't tell people. What we do know for sure is that Amazon's goal is to make money by selling products.

Amazon studies customer shopping habits and design algorithms to encourage buying. No one — except the tight-lipped folks at Amazon — knows what exactly the algorithms are programmed to reward. But, evidence from other authors suggests that the algorithms will push books to readers that are already selling well or selling in an organic growth fashion. The algorithms decide which books Amazon puts in those emails it sends out to readers suggesting they might like to purchase a book. As an author, you'd like the algorithms to work for you. Author Matthias Matting did a study to see how sales impacted the algorithms and posted his research on this on his blog: http://www.selfpublisherbibel.de/test-how-amazons-algorithms-really-work-myth-and-reality. The findings indicate that you need a slow build to get the algorithms on your side. Save your strongest advertisers for last. I know some people suggest doing the opposite — leading with Book-Bub and then having your book be high in the sales ranks to encourage buys on the smaller sites. However, I think the slow build approach makes more sense and will, ultimately, work better.

How do people get on BookBub? Well, my Indies Unlimited colleague Shawn Inmon wrote a great post on maximizing your chances on getting selected by BookBub: http://www.indiesunlimited.com/2014/10/13/bookbub-tips-for-a-successful-submission. The bulk of it comes down to cover. Your cover needs to look like other best-selling book covers. Blurb and reviews are the next most important factors. BookBub says there is no minimum number of reviews it requires, but a lot of authors on various message boards say you need at least 25 reviews to be considered by BookBub. If you look at books featured in BookBub's emails, most have 30 or more reviews. However, some have fewer. If you want your book considered by the Bub, I'd err on the side of having more reviews rather than less. BookBub recently conducted an interview on the online writers' hangout Kboards. The Q&A offers some insights into how the Bub makes its selections. The Q&A is 19 pages, so earmark some time to read this before submitting: http://www.kboards.com/index.php/ topic,204466.0.html.

If you do get the Bub, who do you want to be your lead-up? If you don't get the BookBub, who do you want to try next? Well, after Book-Bub, the three biggest are eReader News Today (ENT), Kindle Books and Tips (KBT), and Pixel of Ink (PoI). All of them have minimum review requirements (usually those reviews have to be posted to Amazon.com).

ENT and KBT both have an eight review minimum. However the KBT eight review minimum is different. In early2015, KBT required a total of eight reviews, and at least four of them had to be "Amazon Verified Purchase" reviews. Verified purchases mean the person bought the book at Amazon and then left a review. If you went to eight different review blogs and they all received a free copy of your book and then left a review on Amazon, none of those would show up as Amazon Verified Purchases. Even though you had eight reviews, you would not be able to get listed on KBT, because four of them aren't verified reviews. I don't know the exact reasoning behind this verified purchase requirement, but it may be due to the review scandal that popped up a few years ago. Several authors were found to have been paying for fake reviews, getting friends to leave positive reviews, and swapping fake reviews with other authors. This caused some to want more veracity in the review process. An Amazon verified purchase review does that. However, if your book is getting more accolades than buyers, it can sometimes be hard to get reviews from purchasers.

One way people in KDP Select boost Amazon Verified Purchase reviews is to do a soft launch of their book. By soft launch, I mean, rather than telling everyone, "Hey, my new book is out right now, please buy it," they publish quietly and make the book free the next day. They then ask those beta readers who've reviewed the book to download the free copy and then leave a review. Free download reviews show up as Amazon Verified Purchases. After that day of free downloads for those in the loop, the author makes wider announcements about the availability of the book. Other than that, there are no author shortcuts to getting Amazon Verified Purchase reviews. You just have to wait for buyers to leave a review. If your book is in Kindle

Unlimited and it is borrowed, that borrower's review will not show up as an Amazon Verified Purchase. Some people have tried gifting a book to a reviewer in order to get it to show up as an Amazon Verified Purchase. Unfortunately, this does not work.

If you're unfamiliar with gifting, Amazon allows you to purchase a book and send it as a gift. The reader will open that gift and download the books at no cost to them. In a gift scenario, the book is purchased at Amazon (by the giver) and then downloaded by another person (the recipient). However, the recipient's review does not show up as verified. If the giver wanted to leave a review, it would show up as a verified purchase (because that person actually made the purchase). Unlike Smashwords, Amazon does not allow authors to give out coupon codes. If you want to give your book away via Amazon, you either have to make it free for everyone or purchase a copy of your book and gift it. If, for some reason, you need to gift copies of your book to someone, it's recommended that you set your book's price to 99 cents and purchase the number of gift copies you need. Then, you can raise the price to the normal amount. Gifts bought at a cheaper price will still be redeemable after the price goes up. It's important to note that if you gift a book via Amazon, the recipient has a right to cash out the gift for an Amazon credit for the value of what you paid. Finally, purchasing gifts of your book will not improve your Amazon sales rank immediately. The rank only moves when the recipient redeems the gift for your book. If the recipient chooses to cash out, then you won't get a sale.

Getting back to advertising sites, the third site I mentioned, POI, has proved useful in getting sales. Unfortunately, POI has been closed to new submissions in recent months. It is not clear when they will reopen submissions, so for them, just keep your eye out. They're worth submitting to, if they're available.

In terms of return on investment, both ENT and KBT are good. Expect between 60 and 200 sales on the day your book is featured on a 99 cent deal on those sites. These are not exact numbers. You could get higher or lower, but based on what other authors have reported about their use of these services, this is a good ballpark range. Don't think because these sites have half a million email subscribers, you'll get a thousand sales. We'll talk about open rates when we get to mailing lists, but most mailers aren't even opened by half of the recipients.

With any of these lists, you have to contend with open rates, busy people and book burnout (people who are excited when they first sign up and buy lots of books, but then realize they'll never read all these books if they keep buying at this rate). The thing to remember about the benefit of any advertising push is that if you get a good bursts of sales on that first day, you'll get some carryover sales over the next couple of days because your book has improved its rank and is, presumably on a category bestseller list. Don't judge your success with an advertiser by just the first day of sales. If you got more than a couple dozen sales, you should move up on some lists and get a few carryover sales the next few days. Only after you've tallied up those sales should you make a decision about whether the advertising is effective or not.

With any place you plan to advertise, subscribe to the newsletter for a while to see if you notice any trends. For example, POI tends to skew toward Christian fiction and romance.

After those guys, who's next? Probably the next two that people say do well are BookSends and The Midlist. These guys are not the big boys, but some authors say they get consistently decent results. A quick word of CAUTION about The Midlist. They have two forms of advertisements — book features (which are free) and custom ads (which costs $100). In some iterations of the website, it was hard to find the free advertising, and only the $100 one was displayed clearly as an option. Definitely make sure you know there are two options available. Most praise has been heaped on the Midlist's free version of advertising.

After those, there are a ton more sites that advertise discount ebooks. These are hit or miss, where some authors see success (in terms of breaking even or doing well), while others see it as a loss because the sales didn't cover the cost of the advertisement. Before advertising, look at the site and check out the advertised books to see what their Amazon ranking is. When you check a book's ranking, check books that were advertised the previous day, as it often takes overnight to see the sales rank spike — especially for sites that send out their email newsletter in the late afternoon or early evening. Here are some of the other sites:

Choosy Bookworm, http://choosybookworm.com
Fussy Librarian, http://www.thefussylibrarian.com
HotZippy, http://hotzippy.net/feature-your-book.html

ReadCheaply.com, http://readcheaply.com/
PeopleReads, http://www.peoplereads.com/
EBookSoda, http://www.ebooksoda.com/
Booktastik, http://booktastik.com/
Read Freely, http://www.readfree.ly/submityourfreebook/
My Romance Reads, http://www.myromancereads.com/advertise

These sites all have various requirements for number of reviews and varying degrees of success.

The final thing I'll say about advertising is that most of these big advertising sites don't want shorter works. Most do not accept short stories, short story collections or novellas. So, if you have a shorter work you're hoping to use as an introduction to your longer, more expensive works, you're going to have trouble advertising it. Some sites, like Booktastik, take shorter works, but their reach is limited, compared to a KBT or ENT.

Pay-Per-Click Advertising

Pay-per-click is a type of advertising where you set an advertising budget and then a site (such as Google, Amazon or Goodreads) shows your ad to customers. While thousands of customers may see your ad, you are only charged when someone clicks it. When the person clicks on your ad, they're often taken to your book's buy page.

There are three places authors commonly do pay-per-click advertising.

Google AdWords. When you search for something on Google, you often see sponsored links (i.e. advertisements) in the results. This is a type of pay-per-click advertising. You see the ad, and that usually counts as an impression. If you click on the ad, then the advertiser has to pay Google. Even though you click on the ad, you may not buy what's on the site that click took you to. The goal of pay-per-click advertising is to drive traffic to your advertising page, where the customer buys the product. Google AdWords uses keywords to determine which search terms the user must search to get your ad displayed. Some people love AdWords advertising and say it's the best thing since sliced bread. However, in order to use AdWords effectively, most people agree you need to be fairly adept at SEO. Don't know what SEO is? Then, AdWords is probably not for you. SEO stands for search engine optimization. It's essentially the practice of using specific keywords to get buying customers to your site. The reason people say not to use Google's pay-per-click advertising unless you're familiar with SEO is because you can use the wrong keywords, and get lots of clicks by people who really aren't your target customers. If you do that, you've wasted your money. Those with SEO experience understand which keywords their paying customers are searching and don't use keywords that bring those who are uninterested in the product. It's hard to figure out what the keywords are that work, and those with SEO experience have some idea. You can obviously learn by doing, but that means you'll likely lose money as you experiment, finding customers who click your ad, stay on your page two seconds and never look back.

Goodreads Ads. Goodreads also offers pay-per-click advertising, but the good news is you're already on a site filled with your target audience, so there is less of a need to understand SEO. All the people on Goodreads are interested in books, so they're already your target audience. You can further target your ad on Goodreads, opting to show your ad to readers who express interest in a specific genre or even specific books (if you write young adult, perhaps you target your ads to Hunger Games readers). You get to design your ad, which usually consists of the book cover and some type of appealing text. Remember when we talked about taglines when creating your book blurb? Well, this is a great place to use tagline text. You pay in advance, and set the amount you want to pay per click (minimum of 10 cents) and the daily limit you want to spend (perhaps $3). Your ad is then shown to users at various times. Goodreads will tell you how many times your ad was shown, calling that the number of impressions you received. You will only be charged when a person clicks the ad. So you might end up with 400 impressions and 2 clicks. Because Goodreads is where readers are, it's worth a try, but it's hard to determine how effective the ads are in terms of garnering sales. If you're only getting five to 10 clicks per day and you normally have one or two sales and the sales rate continues with the occasional 2 to 3 sale day, it's hard to know if the Goodreads ad is the cause or not. Goodreads tells you whether people added your book to their shelf after clicking your ad. That's a good sign if you're getting clicks along with shelf ads.

KDP Select Advertising. As I was putting the finishing touches on this book, Amazon introduced a new pay-per-click advertising option. The advertising was only open to KDP Select users and, of those users, it was not open to erotic material. Under the advertising program, you have to set a minimum budget of $100, but you aren't charged until people start clicking (with Goodreads ads, you are charged the amount you set as your budget in advance). You have to set a minimum budget of 2 cents per click. It's unlikely you'll get an ad at that price because Amazon makes you bid against other would-be advertisers to determine who will get the ad space. The few authors I know who have done it set their bids at anywhere between 25 cents and a dollar. Lower bids were being ignored, and they were generally only getting impressions when they had higher bids. Because it's an auction, Amazon gives you the win at 2 cents higher than the next highest bid. When authors were setting their bids at a dollar, they would only be charged 67 cents if the next highest bid was 65 cents. You have to look at what you're being charged per click to determine what size bids you're winning. Authors I know tended to get a lot more "impressions" than clicks. It's not clear if the impressions improved sales. Because it's all done through Amazon, the company will tell you if the person who clicked the ad actually bought the book, so you do get a sense of the direct correlations between the click and sale. Even though you have to set a minimum budget of $100, people who have used the service say you can terminate your ad campaign at any time. Therefore it doesn't' seem to be a firm monetary commitment, because you're not paying the $100 in advance. This is still brand new, and it is possible Amazon will make some tweaks or authors will find that there are specific ways that work and specific ways that don't work when using this type of advertising. The authors I know did not have the best experience, with most getting more impressions than sales. One author I know said this: "Well, 80,000 impressions, 204 page views and $80 later, I finally sold two [books]. I terminated the ad just now."

Free

Free is an advertising strategy where authors give away a digital book for free. It's a strategy that is abhorred by traditional publishers and has been hotly debated among authors. In this section, we'll explain the reasons authors use free, why it's such a controversial strategy, how to make your book free, and the benefits and drawbacks of free.

So, what's the skinny on free? Giving away your ebook for free is easy to do with data, because it really doesn't cost the author anything to transfer the data. Why would you give away the book you slaved over for free?

Well, the answer is simple: broader exposure. How likely is it that someone is going to take a chance and spend their hard-earned cash on a book by someone they've never heard of? Pretty unlikely right out of the gate. Unless you've got a strong following, super reviews, or word of mouth, your book might languish, being bought by no one.

Many indie authors see free as a gateway to new fans.

However, there's a sizeable chunk of authors who don't like the idea of giving away books for free. First and foremost, they don't want to give away a book they've slaved over, working super hard to get it perfect. They want people to pay for that. I must admit, when I first started publishing, I fell into this camp. I worked hard on that book and I didn't want to give it away for free.

Another reason people, particularly those from a traditional publishing background, give for not liking free is that they feel it devalues books. If you give it away for free, they say, readers will start to expect to pay nothing for books. This argument is by far the weakest. I know, you're asking, "What do you mean?"

Well, let me ask you this, if you had a relative give you an old computer for free, would you assume that all computers should be free? Probably not. What if the company had a deal — everyone who shows up at the store on a certain day gets a free computer (while supplies last)? Would you think that computers should be free because of this? Umm. No.

Free doesn't mean something has no value. Free means we didn't pay money for it. The key with a free promotion is to make the reader realize they got a great deal. The reader who feels that way is likely to buy your next book. After a person reads a free book, you want them to say, "Wow, that was good. I was so lucky to get that for free." Then, you want them to click on the links to other books you've written and start buying them. That is how free works as perfect advertising.

Would you like to know another reason the notion that giving books away for free devalues books is the weakest argument? Because it's a hypocritical argument. Traditional publishers, give books away for free all the time. They send them to reviewers hoping to get the books reviewed. They do this for most books they publish. And the odds of the books getting reviewed, for new, unknown authors, is generally pretty slim. Book reviewers at newspapers, magazines and blogs are deluged with books from publishers. They probably select for review fewer than 10 percent of the books they receive.

Yet, if a self-publisher chooses to take this tactic on a larger scale, assuming they'll get about the same percent read rate, but with average people, not newspapers and reviewers, they're somehow devaluing books. If it's devaluing books for the littles, then it has to be devaluing books for the bigs, no?

Now, with that said, free should not be done willy nilly. If you want to do free and get the most out of it, I would suggest a couple of things.

Don't do free unless you have at least three books. When a person gets a freebie, you want them to buy your other books. You want them to say, "Wow, that was good. Let me get something else." Free works best for the first book in a series. Serial series, where the story isn't finished, work better than series that simply have the same characters in different books. Standalone titles work, too, but just not as well as series. With a serial series, the reader either knows they want to continue the story or not, and purchases the book. With a series that uses the same characters or standalone titles, you have a little more work to do. Readers who like your work might buy something else by you, but you have to convince them first. They have to read the blurb or preview for the next book, and conclude the new book is going to be one they'll like as much or more than the one they just read. A reader who isn't convinced of that won't click to purchase that next book. Freebies tend to work best at boosting sales of the second, third and fourth books in a serial.

Don't make too many things free. While I don't think giving away one or two titles devalues your work, I do think giving everything away for free probably trains your readers to expect your work for free. I would suggest picking one book, one of your better works, to make free, and using that one as the teaser to filter readers to your other works. You can have sales and discounts when you want. But, save free for the thing to bring in paying customers. If you do a lot of series, you can make the first book in each different series free, but I would refrain from offering books two, three or four free.

Advertise free. There are a ton of free books out there, and one way to be found is through advertising. So, advertise your free books, even though it costs money. The follow-through buys of your paid titles should cover the cost of advertising. One author I know has a five-book series, where the first is free. She advertises the free book at least once a month to keep a steady stream of readers coming to it, as the freebie feeds sales to the rest of the series.

How do you make an ebook free? Well, that depends on what type of free you want. Do you want it perma-free (which is short for permanently free)? While perma-free suggests it's permanent, you could at some point return your book to paid by raising the price. Perma-free really is just used as shorthand for a title that you intend to be free for a long time. You cannot do perma-free using Amazon as your sole vendor. People who choose to make their books perma-free do so by going through a distributor, such as Smashwords or D2D. Both those vendors distribute to Apple, Barnes and Noble and Kobo and allow you to set your book's price as free. You cannot set your book's price free when you publish directly to Barnes and Noble (through NookPress); like Amazon, they have a 99 cent price mini-mum. For free, you must use a distributor. Once your book is free on other sites, Amazon will price match your book to free. A recent online discussion suggested Amazon was less likely to price match if the book wasn't also free on the Google Play store. This was someone speaking from anecdotal experience, so it may not be accurate, but FYI. People who use the price-matching method are OK with being free for an extended period.

One thing to remember: when you become free through Amazon price matching, Amazon can take its own sweet time returning your book to normal price. That's why it's called perma-free. It's not some-thing that can be undone quickly. It may, in fact, take several days or weeks. This method is not one to use if you want to have a limited-time sale. To get your free book back to a book selling for 99 cents or more, the first thing you have to do is change the price at the distribu-tor. After that's done, it will take a day (or several days) for that change to reach the vendor sites. Once it gets to the vendors, Amazon has to register the price change at the other site and then change the book's price back on Amazon. Amazon may not register the price change on its own. You can wait a couple of days to see if that happens. If it doesn't, you must alert Amazon that the book is no longer free. Before you alert Amazon, be sure to check all vendor sites where you're pub-lished to ensure the book isn't free anywhere.

If you don't want to use price matching, the only other way to make your book free on Amazon is to join Amazon's KDP Select program.

This means your ebook has to be exclusive to Amazon. It also enrolls your book in the KU and KOLL programs, so readers can borrow your books. If you use this method, your book is only going to be able to be free for 5 days during your 90-day KDP Select enrollment period.

If you don't know if you're going to like free or if it will have value to your book, I'd recommend trying the book in Select for 90 days and doing the five free days. See what kind of bounce your other books get. People who want to try Select should start their book in Select and move it out after 90 days if they are unhappy. Otherwise, the book has to be unpublished at other vendors in order to try Select.

Other Benefits of Free. In addition to getting a sales bounce for your paid books, free books can also help garner reviews and build your mailing list.

Since we're talking reviews, we have to be honest. Reviews on free books can break good or bad, and you never know exactly what you're going to get. The review you want with a free book, is the one we talked about earlier. The reader grabbed it for free, read it thinking, it'll probably be average, but was pleasantly surprised. That person is likely to leave a four or five star review with glowing comments. However, people who pick up books for free are often indiscriminate, picking up things they don't like, thinking, "Hey, I'll give it a try." Sometimes, they're pleasantly surprised. But most times they're not. They'll leave reviews that read like this: "I don't normally read books like this but thought I'd give it a try. I won't be trying any more books like this. It sucked. The plot was shallow. It was stupid...." If the book is good, you're more likely to get reviews on the positive side, but do be aware that free is going to give you reviews from some people who were a bad fit for your book. You will occasionally end up with reviews from people who would never have bought your book and will never buy your books again. That's OK. Bad reviews happen. Move on. Never respond to bad reviews. It never works out well for the author. I'll talk more about author etiquette in Step 6.

Free books can also help you build your mailing list. You can do this in a couple of different ways. On your website, you can offer a free book to anyone who signs up for your mailing list. If you do this, please remember that AMAZON PRICE MATCHES. If the book you offer for free is being sold on Amazon, they may drop your price to free based on this website offer. They probably won't, but you see the occasional post on Kboards about the person it happened to.

The other way to use free to build your mailing list is to put the option to subscribe to your mailing list prominently in the book that is offered free. Put a link in the front matter of the book. Put another link in the back matter of the book. The people who got your book for free and liked it are prime candidates to sign up for your mailing list. They already feel like they got something good for nothing, and they want to give back. A simple way to do that is by signing up for the mailing list. Some people offer a second book or short story free in exchange for signing up for the mailing list.

Drawbacks of Free. Well, I think we've covered all the advantages of making your books free. However, there are drawbacks. I mentioned the negative reviews because of a bad fit in the last section. However, that's minor. One of the main drawbacks of free is that you have to give away a lot of your books to make it work. People like free because it's easy. They are getting a great deal, so people who "buy" free books, tend to hoard. They see it, say, "It's free, so I must grab it now." But, they do this with tons of books. Most people who download your book for free will never read it. The conversion rate on free is fairly low, though I couldn't find great statistics on it. If you check the online message boards, people who offer the first book in their series free tend to say that if 5 percent of the free downloads convert to book 2 sales, that's a good thing. No, you didn't misread that — 5 percent. So, if you give away 100 books, only 5 of those readers (if you're lucky) will like it so much that they go on to buy book 2. Therefore, you have to give away huge numbers to increase your following, because such a small percentage of people will read it and become paying fans.

One author I know did a BookBub and gave away 40,000 copies of a book. The author said the BookBub paid for itself within the day, because the author had sold 475 other titles at full price ($2.99+). This was on Amazon, so the author earned $2 per full-price title sold. That's $950 in sales. The author said the free book would get a slight rankings bump that would lead to more sales of it. While the author was very happy with the BookBub-advertised giveaway, it's very hard to hit those numbers without BookBub. Your free will likely not do well if you only give away a few hundred copies. I ran a freebie under a pseudonym. It had six borrows accrue during the free period, yet when the three-day freebie with 400 downloads ended, the book's sales rank was worse than when I began the free days. The numbers just weren't big enough to do much. I did see a few sales of my additional pseudonym title, but it was only 3 per day for the three days following the free book giveaway.

Mailing Lists

As far as marketing goes, mailing lists are the gold standard. Authors take a lot of time building lists and they are incredibly protective of their list members. At the Virginia Festival of the Book conference, a popular self-published author who'd gone on to get a traditional publishing contract said she refused when the publisher requested her mailing list. She said it was too valuable to just hand over. (See Appendix D Article *Experts Talk Marketing Strategies*)

A big mailing list can help you gain sales. People who are on the list are automatically predisposed to like your work, so sending out a mailer should bring you some sales. The bigger your list, the more sales you're likely to earn.

How do you get the big list? There are entire books devoted to list building. I'm not an expert at list building, so I don't have all the answers. However, I can offer some tips to get you started.

The back matter for your book should include a link to your mailing list Landing Page. That's a special page set up to get readers to sign up for your mailing list. It's sometimes called a Splash Page, too. It should be pretty simple and mainly have the form to fill out their email address, along with a big "SIGN UP" button. If you Google "Splash Page html" or "Landing Page html," you'll get lots of examples and html code you can use to set one up.

One way to improve sign ups via your splash page is to offer something free in exchange for signing up for the email list. Depending on how your mailing list sign up is set up, you can automatically send new signups a free copy of one of your books or short stories. You can have different mailing signup lists depending on where the signups came from.

You can have a contest for something free in exchange for people signing up for your email list. Rafflecopter offers this option. What should you give away? Probably something more neutral that many people would want, such as a $25 Amazon gift card. You can do a giveaway by yourself or join forces with others. I joined a group of authors in sponsoring a giveaway of a Kindle Fire HD or a $100 PayPal credit (winner picked). Almost 240 people signed up for my mailing list in order to boost their chances of winning that top prize. I sent out a separate mailer to the new signups giving them a free copy of one of my books, to thank them for signing up and to introduce them to my work. Only a few remove themselves from the list. Those who stuck with it are potential fans.

Once you have a mailing list, what should you mail them and how often? What you send out should be fairly short. A few news items about what you've been up to in terms of your writing, any new publications — either books or articles, reviews from fans or interesting tidbits fans have sent you. It should be personable and friendly, and put you in touch with the fans. In terms of how often, I'd suggest monthly or every other month. Too often, fans become annoyed and unsubscribe. If the newsletter dates are too far apart, your readers have forgotten they subscribed and may actually unsubscribe, assuming it's junk mail.

Don't just send the message from your author email account. You'll want to sign up with a service that sends emails. MailChimp offers a free account if your mailing list is small. When your list has less than 2,000 subscribers, and you send fewer than two emails per month, you pay nothing. However, if you exceed that amount, you must sign up for a paid plan. Constant Contact also has an email service, but it doesn't have a free option. The advantages you get by using these companies, rather than your business email address, are numerous. First, you're less likely to get filtered as spam. When you have multiple contacts in your "To" or "BCC" field, most public email services (like Gmail or Yahoo) consider that spam. The way these mailing services send their emails is less likely to get filtered as spam because of the multiple recipients. Additionally, if you continue to send messages to multiple recipients, you could get branded by your email service as a spammer. With that in mind, it's probably best to go with a mailing service.

Another good reason to use a mailing service is data collection. These companies can tell you how many people actually opened your emails, and which links people clicked and which ones they didn't. They also give you information to put this into perspective. For example, if 50 percent of your readers actually open the email, you might feel disheartened. However, MailChimp tells you what the industry average is for mailing lists in your category. My newsletter is categorized by MailChimp as media and publishing, and the industry average open rate is 16.8 percent, meaning a 50 percent open rate is pretty good (three times the industry average).

The information these services provide is incredibly valuable in building a newsletter your readers use. If you find that a certain type of link is getting clicked on while others are ignored, then you can include more links like that in the email. If you notice that the links on the first two stories of your email newsletter get clicked on while the rest don't, it may be a sign your newsletter is too long and people aren't getting to the bottom stories. Or it could be a sign that the bottom stories are boring. These companies also tell who your best subscribers are — the ones who open all your emails and click on most of your links. That way, if you're doing a giveaway or looking for readers to reward with a free ARC, you can target the users who are highly responsive to your mailings.

The one thing I will note about these companies is that they require a physical address to include in the outgoing email. They must have this address for legal reasons. Anti-spam laws in the United States require the sender's address to be published. You should get a PO Box for this purpose. PO Boxes are not terribly expensive; they vary per market, but range from $40 - $100 annually. PO Boxes are nice because they offer an address that is not your own real address, and you can pick up mail there. If you have a pseudonym or two, you can set up different accounts using one of these services, but they can each go to the same PO Box.

I have seen a couple of authors on message boards balk at the idea of providing a physical address, and contend it's onerous to get a post office box. Again, I think this is a short-sighted view. Mailing lists really do help you engage your fans, so it's a good idea to use a mailing system equipped to reach the most fans in the simplest way.

Blogs

Some people suggest writing a blog as a way to grow your audience. I would say that a blog can be a good idea, depending on what type of books you write.

For general fiction, I don't know if it's that helpful. Some authors say it works and others say it's not helpful. It's not clear whether blogs will cause fiction readers to purchase your paid fiction. If you write a lot and enjoy posting those shorter works, then, by all means, blog them. Or if your fiction all relates to a specific topic, such as sports or futuristic thinking, and you want to write a blog related to those topics, that's great. However, if you want to focus on your books and aren't interested in writing blog posts on a regular basis, then spending extra time creating a blog isn't a good choice for you.

For nonfiction, blogs can be incredibly helpful. You can use your blog to build a following of readers who are interested in the subject in short bursts, and who will be interested in longer, more substantive work on the subject. A blog can also brand you as an expert in the field or the subject matter over which your nonfiction book is about. Several of the more famous indie writers have built themselves up as experts in self-publishing through their blogs. Both David Gaughran and Jo-anna Penn write fiction, but they have a huge blog following devoted to how to self-publish. To this following, they sell their nonfiction titles on self-publishing.

Authors in other fields who've built a large blog following can do well, both as traditionally published or self-published authors. Bloggers who've gotten traditional book deals include Natalie McNeal, the Fru-galista Files, and Jill Smokler, based on her Scary Mommy blog. How-ever, you don't have to go the traditional route to sell books based on your blog. Rachel Aaron's writing book, *2k to 10k: Writing Faster, Writing Better, and Writing More of What You Love*, was based on a series of blog posts. The book is just 99 cents and does extremely well, often landing in the top 20 of the writing category on Amazon.

If you don't want to write your own blog or wish to write in addition to your blog, you should consider guest blogging. When you guest blog, you write a post for another person's blog. If you're able to guest blog on a blog with lots of viewers, that will put your name in front of a lot of people. How do you guest blog? Believe it or not, it's often just as simple as asking. Only, you can't ask until you know the blog you want to guest on. If you believe the blog has an audience that is com-posed of people who would likely buy your book, that's the blog you want to guest-post on. You should read the blog regularly for a few weeks and comment a few times. As you read the blog, see what kinds of topics the blogger discusses, and figure out what topic you could write about that would complement that. Then, come up with a well thought-out proposal for a guest blog (usually 2-4 sentences) and email the blogger. S/he will either say yes or no. Even if they say no, it may be a very nice no, something like, "Interesting idea but not quite right for my audience. Could you write something that might touch on…?" Almost all bloggers started off exactly how you are — an unknown with little or no following. They understand what it's like, and they're sympathetic to those trying to improve themselves, so long as the person is polite, respectful, and approaches them in a spirit of helpfulness. Sending a brash email saying the blogger needs to publish your post because of XYZ is unlikely to get you anywhere. Respectful and helpful is the way to go. Blogging is a very reciprocal community, so if you share and are helpful, you're likely to get responses in kind.

Blog Tours. In addition to the single, random guest blog, many writers will go on blog tours. This is where you appear on several different blogs over the course of a couple of weeks, usually in the lead-up to a book's release. A blog tour is a writing-intensive task, because they require you to write a blog post (or something else) for every blog you appear on. Not all are cut and dry blog posts. Sometimes you can do an author interview, or a Q&A along with a book excerpt. No matter what you write, it's expected to entertain the reader and entice them to want to know more about you and your books, so that takes effort and time to pull off. Authors can arrange their own blog tours by contacting blogs they think would be a good fit. If you're going to coordinate this yourself, start at least a couple of months in advance of the dates you want and be sure to send the bloggers very coherent proposals for what you will provide their blogs. The bloggers tend to want the blog post a week prior to the date it's supposed to run (so they can schedule it; or schedule something else if you turn out to be a total flake). If all this coordination in addition to writing the posts is too much for you, then you can hire a blog tour company. There are lots of them out there. Just google "blog tour organizer." The fees for this service vary, but some are as low as $50, and they'll coordinate all the blogs for you.

When looking at a blog tour company, or any service provider for that matter, read some online reviews and Google the name to see if you get any negative info. The other thing to concern yourself with is whether the blogs they work with get many hits. If you're doing a blog tour of 10 sites, and each site only gets 150 visitors per month (five a day), then you have to ask yourself if it's really worth all the effort. How can you tell how much traffic a blog gets? There's a company called Alexa (http://www.alexa.com) that ranks websites based on traffic. If you type in any website, you can get its Alexa rank, which will offer a sense of how much traffic the site gets. The basic data is free, but if you want more detailed analysis, you have to purchase that from Alexa. The lower the Alexa number, the better the site is. So a site like Amazon.com has an Alexa rank of 3 in the United States. This means it's the third most visited site in the country. If a website has an Alexa rank in the millions, it's not getting a ton of visitors. That doesn't mean the site is awful. Very good sites may have an Alexa ranking in the hundreds of thousands. But a site with a high rank (lower number) indicates it's getting good traffic.

So that's the skinny on blogs. If you don't love blogging, don't do it. No one will hate you for not having a blog. It takes time and effort to build an audience for your blog and you may not want to put that much into it. I do recommend guest blogging on occasion, as that will help you get your name around to people who weren't necessarily interested in you (as readers of your blog often are).

Social Media

Social media is a big category. These sites are the places people hang out online (where they're, y'know, social). Sites include Facebook, Twitter, Pinterest, Goodreads, Google+, and Tumblr.

Here's the thing. If you're a writer, it's important that people hear about your book. Publishing a book and pretending like it's a secret isn't helpful. You need to have some social presence. The problem many people have is that there are so many options out there for social media, that they try do all of them, and then they do a really bad job at all of them.

Start with one, or maybe two, social media platforms and be there. Interact with people, and enjoy the atmosphere. Readers don't buy stuff from people who endlessly post, "Buy My Book." Posts like that become background noise. Social media is about connecting with readers on a more personal level so they'll be disposed to buy your books when you do occasionally post "buy my book" (or something equivalent). Most social media strategists suggest an 80-20 split for your posts, where 80 percent of it is other stuff and 20 percent is directly related to promotion (i.e. buy my book; my book is available). What is this other stuff you put in the 80 percent? A study found that images performed best (in terms of reach and shares) and questions also improved engagement. When they say images do well, that includes images that are mainly text. I'm sure you've seen inspirational quotes or funny lines as images online. For authors, creating those kinds of images to post can improve your visibility and engagement. One author I know, who wrote a memoir about her life experience and wisdom, is named Pearl and she makes such quotes, calling them "pearls of wisdom." (See *Appendix D, Tips on Sharing Words as Images*, p. 169.)

For those who don't do a lot of social media, let's go over the major players in the social media world.

Facebook. (http://www.facebook.com) Oh, Mr. Zuckerberg, you have reeled me in. This popular network started by Mark Zuckerberg is a place where friends can get together and share aspects of their lives. People connect by adding each other as friends, and commonly post photos, silly things they say, what they're doing at the moment, and news articles. People's own Facebook area is known as their "wall." Whenever they say something they want their friends to see, they post it to their wall. This thing they post is called a "status" or sometimes a "status update." The only thing on a person's wall are things they post, or messages a friend posts specifically to them. When you log onto Facebook, you are typically taken to your "Newsfeed" page. The newsfeed shows the status updates of all your friends, groups you belong to, or pages you "like." (By liking a page, you are agreeing to see its status updates in your newsfeed). If you are a business, such as an author, you will need to create a personal Facebook account for yourself, and afterwards, you can create a Facebook Page in the name of your business (RJ Crayton for me). A page can post status updates to its wall and, in theory, people who have "Liked" that page will see those updates in their newsfeeds. However, Facebook has been trying to figure out how to monetize its business model and has decided that charging business pages is the best bet. Facebook has made it increasingly harder for page content to show up in people's newsfeeds. If you want more people to see your posts, Facebook wants you to pay them more money. There are a lot of people on Facebook, and I would recommend being on it personally so you can connect with other writers in Facebook groups. These groups often have information about new sales and marketing techniques, reader trends, or industry news that can be of use. A few of my favorite Facebook groups for writers are Indie Author Group, Writers Right (where I'm an administrator), and BookGoodies.

In terms of marketing via a Facebook page, it's gotten harder because of the company's push to monetize through business pages. However, many people still do well and engage. The real key to how well a Facebook page works for you is how often you are on it, and how often you are engaging with others. Pages cannot join Facebook Groups, so any interactions of that nature you have to do with your personal account. Therefore, it can be harder to get the level of interaction you'll need, because it's entirely page-based. To improve page engagement, you should definitely use the techniques of images and question-asking. Also, share content from your page to your personal Facebook wall. That will often boost engagement.

Twitter. (http://www.twitter.com) On Twitter, you also make posts which are known as "tweets," and they appear on your feed. Your Twitter feed includes all the tweets of the people you follow on Twitter. Because of this, your feed can be very crowded, and if the people you follow tweet a lot, your feed will move very quickly and you might miss important things said by others.

The main thing with Twitter, like other social media, is to be engaged. If you want to direct a comment at someone, you use the @ symbol plus the person's twitter name. So, people wanting to direct a comment toward me will type, @rjcrayton. Twitter also has something called hashtags (#). You use these if you want to identify the subject or concept of your tweet. People tweeting about books will often use #99cents to indicate the book costs 99 cents or #free to indicate the item is free. Other common hashtags are #books, #amwriting, #thriller, #romance, etc. Don't overdo the hashtags. People prefer one or two hashtags per post and feel like much more than that is excessive.

When someone tweets at you, it's courtesy to respond. You are welcome to respond to any tweet you see on your newsfeed, as people have tweeted it with the hopes of getting a response from someone. Responding to a humorous or useful tweet is one way to build a rapport with others on Twitter. It is common to follow people back if they follow you. This means your feed of tweets will be humongous. It also means your tweets are likely to get lost in the shuffle. If you want your tweets to stand out, they need to be pithy and memorable. Again, pics work on Twitter too, as the network allows you to tweet pictures. When someone likes what you said on Twitter, they will "retweet" or "favorite" it. It's considered good when multiple people retweet your tweets

Pinterest. (www.pinterest.com) This site is all about images. Pinterest is designed to be like an old fashioned corkboard where you pin your favorite pictures, except it's online. As such, your area includes a place for your boards, where you pin your pictures. You can create several boards, each with its own subject, such as food, clothes, recipes, books, etc. Like on Twitter, Pinterest allows you to follow other people and be followed by people. When you log onto Pinterest, you generally appear on your own boards. From there, you can access your pin feed. Like other social media feeds, the Pinterest feed page shows you the pins of all the people you follow. You can like a pin (press the little heart button in the upper right hand corner of the picture) or you can re-pin it to one of your own boards. If your pin is re-pinned, that is considered a good thing.

With Pinterest, you're going to want to have a board about your books (or a board for each book) as well as boards for other interests you might have. Pinterest is wonderful if you have a self-help or advice book. Earlier I talked about images of text. With Pinterest, if you've got great advice or quotes from your self-help book, pin the text as an image (See the Appendix D article on Image Quotes for more info). It's not clear how much pinning help sells books. If your cover is really visually appealing, it will do better than others. I caught sight of what I thought was a stunning cover on Pinterest and clicked through. Like with Twitter, it is not uncommon to follow back people who follow you.

Goodreads. (http://www.goodreads.com) Goodreads isn't what we think of as a traditional social media platform, but it is a social site for booklovers. There, you can join groups, and discuss and rate books. Many of the groups have group reads, where they all agree to read one book and discuss it. If your book gets picked as a group read, that can be a wonderful boon for sales and word of mouth. However, going in and trying to push your book upon Goodreads users doesn't work. To use Goodreads effectively as a social network, you have to be social. You have to discuss books with others and participate in groups like a reader. Then, as time goes on, you'll be able to discuss your writing, and some group members may read your work and pass it on via word of mouth. Another way authors use Goodreads is through its Giveaway program (https://www.goodreads.com/giveaway/new). With that, you can give away one or more physical copies of your book to readers. Goodreads gets all the entry information and selects the winners, so you won't get any subscriber data with a Goodreads giveaway. What you will get is readers adding your book to their To Be Read (TBR) list. Goodreads automatically adds the book to the users' TBR list unless the user clicks a button to refuse. Getting on TBR lists gets your book in front of readers, but only a small fraction of those who sign up for the giveaway will purchase your book if they don't win. As mentioned earlier, Goodreads also has groups that do read for reviews and offers pay-per-click advertising.

Google+. (https://plus.google.com/) Google was one of the last players to join the social media hubbub and Google+ is its entree. The site never caught on in popularity like Facebook. However, Google+ is part of the Google machine, so it can sometimes help your search rankings if you post your blog posts or interviews to your Google+ page. I am not an avid user of Google+, though there are some people who swear by it. If you find your sweet spot in Google+, wonderful, but at this point in time, it's not where people are at.

LinkedIn. (https://www.linkedin.com/) LinkedIn is a network for business people. Generally, you make "connections" with others and then you can keep abreast of their business comings and goings. Some people like to post their blogs to LinkedIn and some people like to network in the discussion groups. At Indies Unlimited, we tried to figure out if there was any value to authors being on LinkedIn, and we couldn't find a whole lot there. However, some people say it's a useful tool for authors. Check out Lynne Cantwell's LinkedIn article. Be sure to read the comments for opinions from those who find it useful.

Tumblr. (https://www.tumblr.com/) This is another social network. It doesn't have as large of a user base as Facebook or Twitter. Its posts are similar to the way Facebook works, and you can build a following there. Tumblr tends to be image heavy, even though it serves as a blog too.

LibraryThing. (https://www.librarything.com/) This site is like Goodreads, but on a smaller, lower-tech scale. The user interface doesn't look as sleek as Goodreads, but it is a community of readers. People chat and discuss books. Authors needing reviews can give away electronic copies of their work in return for a review on this site as well. I must note that I've heard particularly bad things about LibraryThing's read-for-review programs, in that many of the users don't actually leave the reviews. Not one or two, but more than half, which is extremely high.

Instagram. This site is a photo-based social media network. It has 300 million users, and 70 percent of them are outside the United States. People tend to share photos of a personal nature on the site, but it is worth noting that author RM Drake used image quotes to build a successful following and boost sales of his book[32]. The site is mobile-based, so you have to download the app to your phone or tablet before you can use it.

Given how many sites we've listed, it would be really ineffective for you to try to be on all of them actively. Obviously, I think you should have a Goodreads page, as that is listed separately, but you don't need to be an active discussion participant if you don't have time. You can set up your LinkedIn profile, but again, that's not one that requires active participation. Same with LibraryThing. You may simply want to go in and create an author page, so users can find your information and books easily. The rest, however, only join in if you plan to use them. Having a Facebook page that never posts anything is a waste of a connection opportunity. A reader who goes to your Facebook page expects to see regular posts, not a page that no one has been active on for a month.

There are some sites out there designed to help make it easier for you to manage social media. One such site is http://www.hootesuite.com. Through Hootesuite, you can schedule posts to appear on social media sites in advance. The application allows you to connect to multiple social media accounts (Facebook, Twitter, Google+, LinkedIn, Instagram) and post content to all those sites from the same Hootesuite dashboard. You could schedule one status to be posted to all your social networks at the same time, so you didn't have to do it manually. This is great if you just want the appearance of being active on your pages. However, you still have to monitor the responses to any posts you make. Hootesuite has three plans: a free one that allows you to schedule messages for up to 3 accounts, and two paid plans that have varying levels of additional features. The $9.99 monthly plan allows you to connect up to 50 social networks, provides analytic reports, and gives you message archiving. The "Enterprise Plan" appears

---

[32] Tech Times Article, http://www.techtimes.com/articles/31427/20150218/who-is-r-m-drake-how-one-writer-used-instagram-to-become-an-amazon-best-seller.htm

designed for corporations and allows purchasers to connect to unlimited networks. The cost of the Enterprise Plan is not listed.

Marketing Additional Pseudonyms

So now that you've done all this for your main author name, go do it for any pseudonyms that you're writing under too. No, I'm kidding. You don't have time for that. That's why I wanted to briefly discuss marketing when it comes to pseudonyms. Specifically, I'm discussing when you write under at least two names — a main name and a pseudonym. This doesn't apply if your pseudonym is the only name you use for writing.

If you're managing a main name and a pseudonym or multiple pseudonyms, you can't possibly do the same type of social marketing and media for all your names. Given that, pick one name to be your main guy and focus your marketing efforts primarily on that guy. Your main guy gets the Twitter and the Facebook and the Goodreads interaction. That's the one you think you'll make the most money with. Your pseudonym should get an email address, an Amazon Author Page, and a Goodreads page. You can do a website too, if you have time. But depending on how many pseudonyms you have, it might not be efficient to create multiple websites. You want the Amazon Author page so all the pseudonym's books are linked on Amazon and readers can easily find them. You'll want to create a Goodreads Author Page for the same reason. However, the website may be redundant and just one extra thing to keep up with. People who write erotica will often use multiple pen names and that reader is not going to follow them on social media or those kinds of things. However, that reader does want to know all the books the author has written, so you want the Goodreads and Amazon Author pages. Those two pages remain fairly static, only needing to be updated when you add a new book.

Now, if you find you're selling tons more under your pseudonym than your main name, you may want to switch your efforts. That means you would backburner the time-intensive social media (Facebook, Twitter, discussions, engagement) for what was previously the main name, and ramp up those things for the pseudonym (who you'll now call your main squeeze).

I have a pseudonym, and I initially tried to do some of the social media stuff I do with my main name, and found there just aren't enough hours in the day to do that. So, one name is going to have to be there just to sell without tons of marketing help. Yes, you can buy some ads, but you're not going to do a blog tour for a pseudonym if you're just testing the waters with the name or genre.

Holidays

If your book has a tie-in with a holiday, then that's a great marketing thing. Write romances? Then you should really promote them at Valentine's Day. Have a Christmas story? Then promote it at Christmas. If it's a Christmas romance, go for the twofer and promote it at Valentine's Day AND Christmas. When holidays come up, people often are seeking books with similar themes. Got a mother-daughter story? Promote it at Mother's Day. Writing a humor book for expectant fathers? Duh. Father's Day. I'm not sure there's a whole lot more to say about this. Just look for a tie-in and promote the book during that holiday (use marketing techniques discussed above, such as advertising, Twitter, Pinterest, etc.).

Festivals, Public Events

Some authors enjoy going to book festivals, street fairs, and other public events to sell their books. Depending on your personality and the type of book you offer, you can do well. Fiction authors I've spoken to indicated they generally hadn't sold a lot at book festivals and fairs, with 15 books on hand being enough to get them through the day. However, nonfiction authors who are at events that cater toward the subject of their book can do very well. If you have branded yourself as an expert in a subject and speak publicly on it at a public event, that can drive sales to your nonfiction book about the subject. Whether you do public events or not is up to you. It requires being willing to interact with the public in a friendly way. Taking cash at festivals is easy. Some authors also choose to get Square, a free device that allows you to accept credit cards at venues. Square sends you a free swipe device and charges a small percentage of each swiped payment. For more info, visit the SquareUp website, https://squareup.com.

Other Ideas

There are lots of ideas you can use to promote your book. If you want a few of them, I've included a handful of posts I wrote for Indies Unlimited. They're in *Appendix D* (p. 158).

Step 5 Checklist

Web Updates
(After you publish each book, check to make sure you've updated the following places online)

Goodreads

_____ Create or claim book page

_____ Update bio (new writers should add new books)

Author Central

_____ Claimed newest book

_____ Updated bio

Website

_____ Updated book pages to include new book

_____ Updated bio

LibraryThing

_____ Updated book listings

_____ Updated bio

Marketing
Reviews

_____ Email all ARC reviewers with live book page, letting them know they can post review, if book was not set up as a preorder (these are the ARC reviewers from the first checklist, and these are follow-up emails)

_____ Email requests to reviewers for post-publication reviews

_____ Send review copies to people requesting

_____ After one week, follow up with any unposted ARC reviews (if you don't get a response, let it go. You can't make someone review your book)

_____ Follow up with post-publication review requests per their review timeline

Blogging (this is an optional item)

_____ Arrange guest posts

_____ Write your own blog

_____ Participate/Arrange blog tour

Mailing Lists

_____ Created account at mail service

_____ Sent first email newsletter

Advertising

_____ Made a list of advertisers you want to try

_____ Applied to five sites to run a 4-day add blitz, ending with the site you expect to perform the best.

Social Media (check if you chose to join)

_____ Facebook

_____ Twitter

_____ Pinterest

_____ Goodreads

_____ Google+

_____ LinkedIn

_____ Tumblr

_____ LibraryThing

_____ Instagram

Other

_____ Holiday themed promotions

_____ Book or local festival appearances

STEP 6: BE PROFESSIONAL, COURTEOUS

Self-publishing, just like traditional publishing, is a fairly small world. People talk and people get to know each other, even in the context of the online world, so you want to be professional and courteous in all you do online.

If you join online groups for critique or knowledge, always ask questions politely and thank people when they respond. When fans email you, respond to them. They'll appreciate it. If a fan has something negative to say to you, respond in a respectful way that is not argumentative or hostile. If you're not sure how to do that, then just say something along the lines of, "I'm sorry you were disappointed. I appreciate all the feedback I get, positive or negative." That's it. Don't argue with people or try to prove your point. It's generally not worth it, and runs the risk of offending someone who will then go tell everyone they know what an awful person or writer you are. Just like the customer is always right, the reader is always right.

Here are a couple of general rules:

Don't respond to reviews

If you send a reviewer a free copy of your book and they hate it, then, guess what? That's it. There is nothing more to do or say. Do not respond to the review; do not give a point by point rebuttal, explaining why they're wrong or don't get your characters. Keep your mouth shut and move on. The only thing that comes from responding to negative reviews is bad publicity and retaliatory reviews (those posted in order to retaliate for your negative remarks). Big Al, of Big Al's Books and Pals, had an incident with an author who wouldn't stop responding to his review, claiming Al wasn't giving the book a fair shot. It got so bad that other people got her book and started leaving bad reviews and the entire thing attracted so many news reports that it actually has its own Wikipedia entry: http://en.wikipedia.org/wiki/The_Greek_Seaman.

While people can see the danger of responding to bad reviews, people tend to think it's good to respond to good reviews. I would say, if it's simple and polite, "Thank you for reviewing my book," then OK. However, too much more and it looks like you're sucking up or angling for a favorable review of the next book. Some people, as a rule of thumb, just don't respond to reviews. Others only respond in fairly neutral ways. Whichever you choose, don't fight over negative reviews. Don't threaten to sue the reviewer for using your copyrighted book cover to accompany the negative review (yes, someone threatened that: http://www.indiesunlimited.com/2014/08/22/another-badly-behavi ng-author). Do deal with it and move on. In the long run, it's good for your book to have some bad reviews. When people see a book with only five-star reviews, they begin to think something is fishy. A book with lots of five-star reviews and the odd low rating (one- or two-star) indicates it has been read by a wide variety of people and most liked it, but one didn't. As human beings, we know not everyone likes everything, so it sits better with us to see a visual representation of the outlier. As an author, however, every one- or two-star review hurts. We just have to pick ourselves up and get back on the horse. One last note on this subject, however. If your book is getting dinged for actionable items, such as editing, you can update your product description to address the issue. For example, you can get your book re-edited, change the edition number (you can do this when you update your book), and at the bottom of your product description, say "Second Edition has new edits to fix minor grammar problems."

Don't gripe about your fans to your fans.

If you are using social media to communicate with fans and at a loss of what to post, don't post hostility toward fans. Author Chelsea Cain caused much hullabaloo when she posted a comment to Facebook[33] telling fans it wasn't her job to tell them the order of her books or to

---

[33] Screen capture of Facebook comment, https://afterthesucker-punch.files.wordpress.com/2014/09/chelsea-cain_original-comment.jpg

explain how to turn on their "fucking Kindles." Cain received a lot of flak over the comment. Several fans responded to the post saying they wouldn't buy any more of her books, and several people who'd never heard of her before said they would now never buy her books. While some defended the rant as a moment of stress that the online community latched onto to tear Cain down, others thought she was rightly pilloried. No matter which side of that debate you fall on, it's never good when fans feel an author has been disrespectful or willfully unkind to them. It's also not good when the author's Facebook posts, rather than the author's awesome books, become the story. Try to avoid either of those things happening. Often, a rant that would be fine to make to a friend in person is not appropriate for social media. In general, be kind to fans on social media and in public. Save your rants for your spouse or your best friend.

Don't Swap Reviews

It sounds harmless when you first hear it. "Hey, we both need reviews for our books, so let's read each other's books and leave the other person a review." In a world where both people have written fabulous books, this may work out. However, this is not the world we tend to live in. We live in a world where you may swap books and the book you are reading sucks. Then, what do you do? Do you leave that author a one- or two-star review because that's what the book deserves? And then what does that person do in return? Does the one-star author leave your pretty good book a one-star review because you left his book one? The anxiety and drama just aren't worth it.

Don't Talk Trash about Other Authors

This is a recipe for disaster. Specifically, I mean, don't talk trash about other author's work. Their fans get upset, or your fans regard you with a little less respect. One of the worst cases of this involved Lynn Shepherd, who wrote a Huffington Post article saying that JK Rowling should stop writing in order to give other writers a chance at success. She also said she'd never read Harry Potter but thought it was pathetic that adults were reading the series because there had to be much more "stimulating" books out there for adults[34]. Well, within hours, Ms. Rowling's fans had deluged Ms. Shepherd's books with

[34] Lynn Shepherd JK Rowling article, http://www.huffingtonpost.co.uk/lynn-shepherd/jk-rowling-should-stop-writing_b_4829648.html

one-star reviews, many of them starting with, "I didn't read Ms. Shepherd's book, but…." Now, Ms. Rowling did not ask for this, but her fans were incensed on her behalf and decided to teach Ms. Shepherd a lesson. You don't want to be taught a lesson by other writers' fans. Nor do you want to offend other writers unnecessarily. If you don't like a writer's books, keep your mouth shut about it. However, do feel free to praise any authors you adore.

Don't Miss Deadlines or Turn in Sloppy Work

If you are going to write a guest post for another blog, get it done on time. Use your calendar (whether online or in paper) and insert the item that's due on your calendar, along with a reminder the week before it's due. That way you'll make sure to get it done. Also, don't turn in sloppy, typo-riddled work to anyone. If someone is letting you guest post on their blog, they don't want to spend excessive time editing your work. They want it to be clear, coherent, and relatively error free. We all make mistakes, but you should strive to hand over flawless work. Also, don't miss deadlines you set for publication. If you tell your fans the book will be published on X date, get it done by that date. You can always give a later date with the goal of moving up the release date. But try not to push it back.

Not All Authors Are Above the Fray

While I've tried to offer some advice about professionalism to help keep you above the fray, not everyone likes to be above it. I'll just take a moment to note that one reason to let things go and be professional is because people have long memories. If you do something they don't like, they may try to get you back. I mentioned retaliatory reviews in reference to review swaps and Lynne Shepherd, who received retaliatory reviews from fans. These are not the only instances in which people leave retaliatory reviews. Many authors do not leave reviews under their author name, or only leave reviews under their author name if the review is three stars or higher. Often, they do this because they're authors, and they know that one- and two-star reviews hurt. They also do it to avoid retaliatory reviews by the author or the author's friends and relatives. Authors who have received bad reviews on Amazon have been known to ask friends and family to vote down the bad review. (There's a button beneath all Amazon reviews that asks if the review was helpful and people can vote Yes or No.) Unhappy authors have also left a negative review on other author's books and asked friends to vote the negative review up. Reviews are small potato things. You'd hate to get on someone's bad side because of carelessness or sloppiness, and miss an important opportunity. Most authors are very kind and generous, but be aware that, like in any part of life, you may encounter some who are mean-spirited and vindictive.

Step 6 Checklist

_____ Be courteous, professional

_____ Respond to fans in timely, friendly way

_____ Say no to review swaps

_____ Avoid online griping

_____ Turn in work on time

STEP 7: COLLECT DATA, ASSESS, ADJUST

This is the final step of the process and one that a lot of self-publishers forget to do. They do the first six steps, have results they're not happy with, but they just keep going. It's imperative to collect data about your progress, assess it and adjust your approach, if necessary.

Let's say that for your first book, you decide to go into Amazon's KDP Select program, where you are exclusive to Kindle and are part of the Kindle Unlimited program (where readers can borrow your book). If you participate in the program for 180 days (two terms) and have only three borrows and few sales, guess what? That program isn't doing a lot for you. Consider pulling the book from Select and publishing it on the other platforms.

Let's say that you weren't interested in doing free; it rubbed you the wrong way. However, now you've published three books in a series, and the series as a whole still isn't selling. Enough with the 99 cent deals and random discounts; try making book one perma-free. If you're not selling, it can't get worse. Try something different.

In order to assess and make decisions, you'll need to do a couple of things. The first and most important is to look back at your goals. We talked about determining your goals up front. Why did you decide to self-publish? Is it just to get that book out there so people can read it? If that's the case, then maybe your job is done. If this is the only book you have in you, and you want it to do well, then assess your progress on that book alone. You have to try strategies that focus only on selling that book, because that is the only one you plan to write. If your goal is to make money self-publishing and you're not making any money, then your assessment and adjustments are going to focus on implementing that overall strategy, and may involve tinkering with some or all of your book catalog.

At this point in the process, look at your original goal and then write down the benchmarks you think will be necessary for you to achieve your goal. If your goal was to publish a book, the benchmark is pretty singular: is the book published? If your goal was to publish a book and have moderate success with it, that's a lovely but vague goal. You need to now set your benchmarks to define what moderate success is. While you should come up with a number of books sold for part of your goal (perhaps selling one book per day for an average of 30 books per month), you should also include non-numbers items too. The thing with setting goals is that you need to set goals for things you can control. Unfortunately, you can't control the number of books you sell. You can control how many guest posts you offer to write. You can control the advertising you select to purchase (in most instances). You can control the number of review requests you send out. You can control the time you spend on social media. You can control your keywords and your cover. You need to pay attention to the sales numbers, to make sure the benchmark goals you set are things that contribute to increasing those sales number. But, you need to focus your benchmark goals on thing you can actually control.

If your numbers goal for moderate success is selling seven books per week, you'll need to set some non-numbers goals too. Perhaps you'll choose new keywords for your book. That's an actionable, measurable benchmark you can set and easily check off your list when it's done. After it's done, you can watch your sales chart and asses to see if changing the keywords had an effect.

If your goal is to make enough money as a self-publisher to quit your job, then you need to come up with that number goal. How many books per day or per month will you need to sell to do that? That number is probably going to be big, and probably nowhere near what you're selling right out of the gate. But don't worry about that if you're in this for money making. For money-making, this is a long-term goal, and you're going to use that big number as your FINAL GOAL. You're going to set up a bunch of smaller, much more doable "stepping stone" goals along the way that are going to get you to your FINAL GOAL eventually.

Once your benchmarks are set, you can collect data to assess where you are and where you need to go. If your goal was to make enough money to quit your job, and you're selling one 99 cent book per week (averaging four books per month), then you have a long way to go. But, remember, that's OK. You'll get there over several books, because that's how the big publishers do it. So, first up, let's look at the type of data we want to collect to assess where we're at. Create some spreadsheets for the following data:

Book Sales

How many books are sold at each vendor per month? I suggest you have a section for each book you have for sale. The rows should be the months (Jan-Dec.). Columns should include the Vendor, the number of units sold and, if applicable, the number of borrows or free units downloaded. If you have a book that's perma-free, you'll just have the number of free downloads. You should have a total at the bottom of the section (just after the month of December), for total number of books sold or given away. This gives you a spitball number of how you're doing for the year. Your next two columns should be called Marketing, followed by Notes. In that marketing slot, note if you did any marketing that month and what it was (guest blog, advertising, discounted book price). If you notice a spike in sales one month, you'll be able to see if your marketing effort contributed to it. If you notice a sales spike and you did no marketing, then it's time to think about what might have contributed to your sales blip. If you have an inkling as to what caused the sales bump, make a note of what it was in the Notes column. Let's say you did no advertising, but your book is on the spread of a deadly virus and there was an Ebola outbreak that month. Mention that in your Notes column. That's a reasonable guess as to why your virus book suddenly had a boost in sales. At the end of the data collection section, I link to sample spreadsheets to help you visualize how the spreadsheet should look.

Expenses

Keep track of your expenses. This is obviously helpful at tax time. But, it's also helpful just to see where your money is going. You'll want to include info any time you buy a cover, cover art, editing, advertising (see next note), CreateSpace proofs, Goodreads giveaway hard copies, web hosting, domain names, etc. Anything you are spending money on, you should keep track of here. If there's ever a time when you feel expenses are too high, this is a great spreadsheet where you can look and see where to cut expenses. It can also help you notice when you have encroaching expenses. For example, many web hosts charge a low introductory rate and then jack up the price for year two. If you notice this in your expenses, you can decide if it's worth your time and energy to pick a domain host that's cheaper.

Advertising

Keep track of advertising results on a spreadsheet. This will help you make decisions about which advertisers work for your books and which ones don't. While I suggested some advertisers earlier in this book, that's not a definitive list. Also, some advertisers work better for some genres than others. Other authors may love a site that worked horribly for your books. If that's the case, make a note so you don't advertise there again. In the advertising spreadsheet, in the rows, list the advertiser names. In the columns, you'll want to keep track of the book sales for the book advertised on the day of your promo, the day after, and the days following. Following those columns, you may also want to track sales of any related books. So if you're advertising book one of a series, you should also track related sales of book two for the weeks following the sale. You want to monitor it for a couple of weeks because people take time to finish books. You'll get some who devour book one immediately, but others who take a little time with it, but still move on to book two. If the discounted book sales don't cover the cost of the ad, but you find that sales for book two in the series take off, then the advertisement may still be worth it because of the carryover sales. Also, don't forget to include your mailing list as an advertisement. Every time you send out an email newsletter that contains book links or a call to action from your fans, track book sales to see whether that newsletter made an impact. Often times, mailing lists are the most effective form of advertisement.

I'm going to take a brief detour here to mention Google Alerts [35] and Mention.com [36]. These are both ways you can track mentions of your author name or book names online. Each service allows you to enter book names or author name to track each time the name is mentioned

[35] Google Alerts, https://www.google.com/alerts
[36] Mention.com, https://en.mention.com/

online. I have a Google Alert set for RJ Crayton, and each time that is mentioned, I get an email from Google with a link to where the name was mentioned. A sudden, inexplicable, surge in sales is sometimes explained with a Google Alert email showing you were the book club selection of some online group. Google Alerts is a free service and you can create multiple alerts with it, while Mention.com is free for a single alert, but costs money for multiple alerts.

Getting back to assessment and analysis, the thing to remember is that data is your friend. You don't want to spend all your time looking at data. You have books to write, advertising to schedule, and a ton of other things you can be doing with your time. However, sit down at least once a month and look at the numbers for the previous month to see how things are going.

When you have the data in place, you can see how things are working. Did a change in keywords do anything to boost the sales of your books? Give it a couple of weeks to take effect when you make a change like that. But, make a note in your notes column and see what happened to book sales. What about a guest post? Did the guest blog on the site with the great Alexa rating lead people to purchase your book or sign up for your mailing list?

Certainly look at your sales numbers after any changes you make to your book listings or any publicity or advertising you do. But you don't have to load and reload your sales numbers everyday if that's not the type of person you are. You'll want to give things a chance to work. Looking at your data monthly gives you a trend for the month so you can see where things stand. You don't have to make changes every month based on the data, but you need to know where you are at the end of each month.

If the data's been somewhat up and down, give it three months to see if a trend of no sales or depressed sales continues. If so, try a new strategy to jumpstart things. If you're happy with the way things are going for a certain book, then just let them be. You don't have to do anything with that book; only make changes for ones that aren't selling. Similarly, if you want to try a new strategy for your books, you don't have to try it with all the books. Try it with one book to start, and if it works there, expand the strategy to see if it works with other books. Once you have strategies in place that lead your books to sell more often than they don't sell, then you are in the zone. Enjoy it.

Let's take a brief look at some real-world assessments you might make. Let's say your goal was moderate success and you defined that as 30 copies per month, averaging one sale a day. When you started you were selling five copies per month at $2.99 per ebook.

One thing you could do to see if your sales numbers improved would be to lower the price. Maybe you drop your price to 99 cents and see what happens.

If you drop your price to 99 cents for a month, and in that month have 12 sales total, then that price drop has more than doubled your sales. Unfortunately, that is still less than half of your goal. Next you may want to try an advertisement, guest blogging, or seeking reviews on review sites.

If you do all those things and sales still don't increase, then you may want to consider changing your keywords, blurb, or cover. We talked earlier about these things when you were first doing them. The hope was to get them right the first time. But sometimes it doesn't always work out that way. If a book isn't selling, changing keywords or a blurb are easy things to alter to see if you get better results. As with any type of experiment that you want to be somewhat scientific, don't alter too many variables at once. If you think better keywords would get more people to your book, change the keywords. Don't necessarily change the blurb and the cover at the same time (unless you've gotten feedback that they're all rotten). If people tell you they picked up your book despite the cover, that's a sign that it's a bad cover for your genre. I didn't say it was a bad cover. I said it was a bad cover for your genre. Sometimes even a good cover can send the wrong message to potential readers. If you're getting comments indicating your cover is unappealing or sends the wrong message, it might be time to change the cover and see if that improves sales. Lastly, if your cover is working and the keywords seem fine (unfortunately, Amazon gives us no data on whether keywords are driving readers to the book), then perhaps it's your blurb. Try something new if people tell you the blurb isn't exciting them about the book. Experts say to give keyword changes about a week to take hold and start driving traffic (or not driving traffic, if you've picked incorrectly) to your book.

Unfortunately, the feedback you get on the blurb and cover will all be anecdotal. It will just be randomly given by people who want to tell you, which is not the most scientific way to go. If you really think it's your cover or blurb, you can try to solicit some input from others (try your mailing list or some online groups). Short of those strategies, you won't have a lot of data on the cover or blurb, and you won't know if changing them will improve sales until you actually do it. If you do change covers or blurbs, get some feedback on the new ones before you make the switch. See if they resonate with readers.

Getting back to those people who are in it for the money. I mentioned earlier that you'll want to benchmark with smaller goals. Your small goal may initially be the same as the person who wants moderate success: selling 30 books per month of a title. You'll do the same thing that person does, but presumably you'll be doing it with more books. If one book is the strongest book in your arsenal, you'll want to benchmark higher sales expectations for that books than for weaker books. If you're writing a series and plan to go perma-free once book three is done, then your assessment and resulting strategy might be somewhat different. If your series isn't finished and your strategy is series writing, it behooves you to only change things like keywords, blurb, or cover, and advertising, rather than trying to write a guest blog. Your writing time should be spent finishing the series, so you can implement your overarching strategy. Your benchmarks with several books may be slightly less specific. You might say for your benchmark number goals that you want one book to be selling 50 copies per month, another 20 copies per month, and another 10 copies per month, for an overall total of 80 per month. You won't necessarily care which book is the high seller, so long as one of them is.

If your strategy is perma-free as a lead in, and you find that very few people go on to purchase book two (somewhere in the .05 percent range, rather than the 3 to 5 percent range), then you may need to look at your free book and give it a rewrite. Or, if you have a lot of people pick up book two after reading the free book one, but almost none of those book two readers buy book three, then you may have to look at the content of book two. Whatever your strategy is, you need to look at whether it is working, and if it's not, assess what could be causing it to not work. That's the only way you're going to have success: by taking a critical look at what's working and what's not. In the end, you need to jettison approaches that aren't working and keep the approaches that are.

Sample Spreadsheets

You can find sample spreadsheets for Book Sales, Expenses, and Advertising at http://rjcrayton.com/sp/samples. This is a link for book purchasers, so please don't share it.

Success Stories

At the beginning of this book, I promised you some success stories. So, who are some successful self-publishers and what kind of journeys did they have?

Well, let's look at two of the top names: Amanda Hocking[37], who was dubbed the "99 cent millionaire," and Hugh Howey, author of the *Wool* saga.

By all accounts, Hocking loved reading and writing, and she wrote a lot. In fact, Hocking wrote so much she had stockpiled 17 manuscripts. She'd sent several manuscripts to agents, but had not been able to get one to take her on as a client. According to The Guardian[38], Hocking decided to self-publish in order to earn enough money to see a traveling exhibit on Jim Henson and the Muppets. Lucky for Amanda that she had all those books lying around. In April of 2010, she published her vampire novel, *My Blood Approves*. After two weeks she was selling nine copies per day, so she decided to upload some more of her works — I mean she had 17 of them (all rejected by agents). Over the next year, she published eight more novels.

That sounds almost like a real publisher, doesn't it? Don't just publish one and wait. Publish a lot. Nine titles over a one-year period is a lot for a single author. And they weren't nine pieces of junk she'd thrown together. These were novels she'd written over a several year period and been told they weren't good enough. Hocking had practice on her side, and she had volume. These are the things that make success in publishing. There's a little bit of luck involved, too. But in order to have that lucky strike hit, you need to have the quality output, and Hocking did. By the end of that year, she'd sold over a million copies of her novels, most of which were series. She'd price the first at 99 cents and charge more for later titles (which is why she was dubbed

---

[37] Amanda Hocking Wikipedia page, http://en.wikipedia.org/wiki/Amanda_Hocking#Bibliography
[38] Amanda Hocking profile in The Guardian newspaper, http://www.theguardian.com/books/2012/jan/12/amanda-hocking-self-publishing

the "99 cent millionaire").

Hocking's journey, given what we know about self-publishing, makes perfect sense. Though, her journey was fairly quick. Let's turn our attention to someone else, someone who had a slower build, someone whose journey is probably more what people might expect: Hugh Howey. Now wait a minute, you're saying. *Wool* was an overnight success. He uploaded it and was soon selling 3,000 copies a month, right?

Well, yes, *Wool* was an overnight success. It's just that *Wool* wasn't Howey's first book. Howey discusses his pre-Wool success in this Tech Crunch piece[39]. Prior to publishing *Wool*, Howey had been at the self-publishing game for three years, and he'd published six novels that had sold about 5,000 copies. That's about 1,600 books per year, over the three year period. If we assume that each book sold at $2.99 and he earned $2 per copy, that's $3,200 in book income per year for three years. While many self-publishers would be ecstatic to earn that amount, the income was not enough to live on. I'm not sure anyone would call Howey's early sales figures a roaring success.

But, here's the thing, when *Wool* came out, Howey had six other books that *Wool* lovers could go read. He had a built-in backlist. That's one of the wonders of publishing, whether it's self-publishing or traditional publishing: readers love a known quantity. If they like your work, they'll go buy more of it. At press time, Howey had more than 18 self-published works on sale. *Wool*, as his break-out success, feeds readers to his other works.

Let's look at another success story: Joe Konrath. Now, he's not quite your typical self-publishing success story because he wasn't some guy who came out of nowhere. Konrath had been published traditionally and was what you call a midlist writer. He wasn't super famous, but enough people had heard of him and bought his books that it was profitable for the publisher to keep publishing him. Joe decided to try self-publishing some things his publisher didn't want. And, lo and behold, those titles did really well. Joe began publishing his backlog of stuff his traditional publisher hadn't been interested in, as well as a few new items. His sales took off, and he eventually dug into his own pocketbook and bought back the rights to titles he'd previously sold to publishers. I mention Konrath because he is one of the most transparent

---

[39] Tech Crunch interview with Hugh Howey, http://techcrunch.com/2014/05/19/hugh-howey-author-of-the-silo-saga-talks-about-making-it-big-in-self-publishing/

people ever about self-publishing. So transparent, he gives you his sales numbers. Konrath is a great success story because he shows how the number of books you publish really ads up and is what really helps you start to be profitable in publishing. To see Konrath's earnings, visit his website here: http://jakonrath.blogspot.com/2013/10/guest-post-by-tom-keller-and-konrath.html. The chart is organized by title and year. The thing to note is, in 2009, Konrath published 10 books. His weakest seller, a book called *Dumb Jokes*, sold 408 copies, while his strongest seller, *The List*, sold 7,129 copies. In the following year, Konrath had a total of 20 books published (10 from the previous year and 10 for 2010). His weakest seller was a title called *Banana Hammock*, which sold 597 copies. *The List* was still his strongest seller, with 16,212 copies sold (more than double the previous year). His third biggest seller for 2010, *Trapped*, was a new publication that year. The Konrath chart, if you break out the numbers, is a great lesson in the power of multiple titles. He has some that do poorly and some that are power-houses. The key is to get enough titles out there that, overall, you are profitable. Just like traditional publishers do.

If you're looking for other self-publishing success stories, check out this Kboards page: http://www.kboards.com/authors. It lists the most successful self-published authors, including the total number of books they've sold in their self-publishing careers and the number of titles they've published. HM Ward, the leader, has sold more than 5 million copies of her 37 published titles. She's been publishing since 2011. Howey and Hocking are on the list too. Each has sold more than 1.5 million books. Howey's been publishing since 2009 and has 18 titles, while Hocking started publishing in 2010 and has 17 books. Go ahead and peruse the list. The thing you'll notice about the top earners is they have a lot of published titles under their belts. They provide volume and good quality their fans enjoy. If you want to reach monetary success, these are the folks to emulate.

Step 7 Checklist

_____ Book Sales spreadsheet

_____ Advertising spreadsheet

_____ Expenses spreadsheet

Goals

_____ Created overarching goal

_____ Created benchmark goals

_____ Assess progress

_____ Make adjustments

YOUR STORY

Well, , our part of the journey together has to come to an end. You've been given an overview of all the things you need to succeed in self-publishing. You've figured out your goals, written a good book, polished it professional, published it, marketed it, been professional, and are now collecting and assessing your data so you can make the necessary adjustments. You rock!

OK, perhaps I'm getting ahead of myself. You've read the book, which means you rock! Next, you'll be implementing the steps, and hopefully publishing a fabulous book in the near future. You have everything you need to be successful. This is the end of the main part of the text. What follows are supplemental items that will help you on your journey.

First up are checklists. I'm a list person, so I love lists and find it really helpful to have checklists. The checklists section compiles the checklists I put at the end of the sections in one spot. (In fact, the checklists were only in the appendices originally, but a beta reader though they'd be helpful further up). The checklists are a quick visual representation of what's in the book preparation steps.

In addition to liking lists, I also like quick reference guides. So, rather than thumbing (or in this instance, clicking) through the book to find suggested cover designers, book review sites, or other items, you can just check out Appendix B. It's a list of websites and service providers that were referenced within the text of the book.

At some point during the editing phase, I realized there were a lot of acronyms in this book. I've been doing self-publishing for a while so they roll right out of my mouth now, but they didn't always. Therefore I threw in Appendix C to cover acronyms and self-publishing terms. It's a quick guide that you can glance at if you're trying to remember what a specific acronym means.

The final appendix, D, is a bunch of my Indies Unlimited articles.

The first two articles offer some tips that are helpful in the actual writing of books. The remaining articles focus mainly on marketing tips related to your books, author brand, and author website. The last two articles relate to something that's not often talked about on self-publishing blogs: how to deal with your intellectual property (your books) after you die. These are useful to read over so you know the issues, and are able to act when you're updating your will or choosing to establish a limited liability corporation (LLC). These articles are great to read as you get into marketing your books and are looking for more ideas than what were mentioned in the body of the book.

And I think that is about it for me. Good luck with getting your book (or books) published.

After your book is up and for sale, drop me a line (http://rjcrayton .com/contact). Seriously, send me a message and a link to your book page. I love to hear success stories and am always looking for a good read. I promise I'll respond back to offer a word of congratulations.

We've come as far as we can together. The rest of this journey is on your shoulders, but know that it's been great riding shotgun so far. Best of luck to you.

-RJ Crayton

APPENDIX A: CHECKLISTS

I've compiled all the checklists at the end of the chapters into one spot. If you would like to print the checklists for yourself, you can get a printable copy in PDF or Microsoft Word (in case you want to change one or two items) on my website at http://rjcrayton. com/sp/samples. Please do not share this link, as it for book purchasers.

Step 1 Checklist

_____ Determine your goal (what you want from self-publishing)

_____ Write down your goal

Step 2 Checklist

Writing Good Books

_____ Set writing habit goal

_____ Determined what you plan to write about

_____ Evaluated work ideas/actual work for accountability issues

_____ Decided if you will use a pseudonym

_____ Checked to see whether author name is already in use

Beta Readers

_____ Identified beta readers willing to read

_____ Cleaned up manuscript to best of your ability (thorough read through and spell check)

_____ Sent manuscript to beta readers with questions

_____ Received beta feedback

_____ Nudged beta readers who did not respond

_____ Thanked beta readers

_____ Incorporated changes based on beta reader feedback

Time releasing

_____ Determined if this strategy is for you, and if so, created a schedule that works for you

Step 3 Checklist

Editing

_____ Substantive editor (optional)

_____ Copy editor

_____ Proofreader (either hired or done yourself)

Cover

_____ Created or bought ebook front

_____ Wraparound cover (ordered for later or plan to make)

Blurb

_____ Blurb written

_____ Tagline written

Step 4 Checklist

Front Matter

_____ Copyright Page

_____ Title Page

_____ Dedication

_____ Active TOC

_____ Review Quotes*

_____ Subscribe Request*

Back Matter

_____ Book Preview

_____ Leave a Review

_____ Acknowledgements*

_____ About the Author

_____ Also by Author

_____ Subscribe Request*

_____ Review Quotes*

_____ Book Club Questions

Formatted Book For:

____Smashwords

____Draft2Digital

____Amazon

____Apple iTunes^

____NookPress

____CreateSpace

____Google Play^

_____All Romance ebooks^

_____Libiro^

^ You cannot submit Microsoft Word files to these companies. You will need a formatted epub (or possibly PDF) document.

Pre-Publish Items

_____ BISAC categories selected

_____ Keywords selected

_____ Price selected

_____ Reviewed book preview

_____ ISBN for print

_____ Email account created

_____ Bank account established

_____ Registered Copyright

Published To:

_____ Amazon

_____ Google Play

_____ Libiro

_____ All Romance ebooks

_____ Kobo

_____ Barnes and Noble

_____ Apple

Smashwords

_____ Smashwords Store

_____ Kobo

_____ Barnes and Noble

_____ Apple

_____ Oyster

_____ ScribD

_____ OverDrive

_____ Page Foundry

_____ FlipKart

_____ Library Direct

_____ Baker & Taylor

Draft2Digital
_____ Kobo

_____ Barnes and Noble

_____ Apple

Print
CreateSpace
_____ Amazon

_____ Expanded Distribution

_____ Lulu

_____ Lightning Source's Ingram Spark

Step 5 Checklist

Web Updates
(After you publish each book, check to make sure you've updated the following places online)

Goodreads
_____ Create or claim book page

_____ Update bio (new writers should add new books)

Author Central
_____ Claimed newest book

_____ Updated bio

Website
_____ Updated book pages to include new book

_____ Updated bio

LibraryThing
_____ Updated book listings

_____ Updated bio

Marketing
Reviews
_____ Email all ARC reviewers with live book page, letting them know they can post review, if book was not set up as a preorder (these are the ARC reviewers from the first checklist, and these are follow-up emails)

_____ Email requests to reviewers for post-publication reviews

_____ Send review copy to people requesting

_____ After one week, follow up with any unposted ARC reviews (if you don't get a response, let it go. You can't make someone review your book)

_____ Follow up with post-publication review requests per their review timeline

Blogging (this is an optional item)

_____ Arrange guest posts

_____ Write your own blog

_____ Participate/Arrange blog tour

Mailing Lists

_____ Created account at mail service

_____ Sent first email newsletter

Advertising

_____ Made a list of advertisers you want to try

_____ Applied to five sites to run a 4-day add blitz, ending with the site you expect to perform the best

Social Media (check if you chose to join)

_____ Facebook

_____ Twitter

_____ Pinterest

_____ Goodreads

_____ Google+

_____ LinkedIn

_____ Tumblr

_____ LibraryThing

_____ Instagram

Other

_____ Holiday themed promotions

_____ Book or local festival appearances

Step 6 Checklist

_____ Be courteous, professional

_____ Respond to fans in timely, friendly way

_____ Say no to review swaps

_____ Avoid online griping

_____ Turn in work on time

Step 7 Checklist

_____ Book Sales spreadsheet

_____ Advertising spreadsheet

_____ Expenses spreadsheet

Goals

_____ Created overarching goal

_____ Created benchmark goals

_____ Assess progress

_____ Make adjustments

APPENDIX B: SERVICE PROVIDERS

While I listed service providers for covers, etc., in the text of the book, sometimes I think it's nice to have a handy reference page, rather than having to search through the text for the piece of info you need. So, here, I'm compiling the lists of service providers that were elsewhere in the book.

Vendors /Distributors - places to sell your books:
- **Smashwords:** http://www.smashwords.com/about/how_to_publish_on_smashwords
- **Draft2Digital:** http://www.draft2digital.com
- **Amazon Kindle Direct Publishing KDP** (eBooks): http://kdp.amazon.com
- **Barnes and Noble**: http://www.nookpress.com
- **All Romance eBooks**: https://www.allromanceebooks.com/publishers.html
- **Libiro**: http://www.libiro.com/index.php?route=information/information&information_id=9
- **Google Play**: https://play.google.com/books/publish
- **Apple**: http://www.apple.com/itunes/working-itunes/sell-content/books/book-faq.html
- **Kobo**: http://www.kobo.com/writinglife
- **Amazon CreateSpace** (paperback): https://www.createspace.com/
- **Lulu** (hardcovers): http://www.lulu.com
- **Lightning Source** (hardcover or paperback): www.lightningsource.com

Formatting Guides:
- **Publish on Amazon Kindle with Kindle Direct Publishing** by Kindle Direct Publishing (FREE ebook): http://www.amazon.com/dp/B004LX069M/
- **Smashwords** Style Guide (FREE download): http://www.smashwords.com/books/view/52
- **Nookpress Style Guide:** http://cp-barnesandnoble.kb.net/kb/article?ArticleId=4339&source=Article&c=12&cid=28
- **Draft2Digital Style Guide**: https://www.draft2digital.

com/styleguide/

Beta Readers:

Ideally, you'll find beta readers among people you know, but if you don't have a wide circle that you can count on to read, you can go online. Try these forums for beta readers, if you feel comfortable with people you haven't met. Hang out in the group and see who might be a good fit for you. Remember, reciprocity is important. Also, follow the group's rules.

- **Goodreads Beta Reader Group,** https://www.goodreads.com/group/show/50920-beta-reader-group
- **World Literary Group Beta & Critique Group,** http://www.worldliterarycafe.com/forum/125
- **Absolute Write Beta Readers,** http://absolutewrite.com/forums/forumdisplay.php?s=0cd99b5072c45e00673dd608ae56bde1&f=30

Editing Sources:

- **PeoplePerHour,** http://www.peopleperhour.com. This site is not just for editing, but on it, you can find editors willing to edit your work for discount prices. As always, caveat emptor (let the buyer beware). Check ratings, references before purchasing.
- **Indie Author Group on Facebook:** https://www.facebook.com/notes/indie-author-writing-group/editors/350443775117301. This file lists the services of some editors, some of whom have low prices, such as $.0048 per word.
- **Editing by Rebecca,** http://www.editingbyrebecca.com

Cover Art:
- **Indies Unlimited Do-It-Yourself Primers**
    o **Book Comparisons** http://www.indiesunlimited.com/book-cover-comparison-page/
    o **Cover Basics** http://www.indiesunlimited.com/2014/12/23/basic-elements-of-digital-book-cover-design

- **Purchase Covers** (sites that offer pre-mades, personal and CreateSpace covers)
  - Go On Write, http://www.goonwrite.com (pre-mades $40)
  - Yocla Book Covers, http://yocladesigns.com/pre-made (pre-mades start at $35)
  - Graphicz X Designs, http://graphiczxdesigns.zenfolio.com/f641008928 (pre-mades start at $30)
  - The Book Cover Designer, http://thebookcoverdesigner.com/ (pre-mades start at $30)
  - Alchemy Book Covers, http://www.alchemybookcovers.com/ (you-pick-the-image covers start at $50; pre-mades $65)
- **Licensed Cover Art**
  - Wiki Commons, http://commons.wikimedia.org/ (free)
  - Pixabay, http://www.pixabay.com (free)
  - Period Images, http://www.periodimages.com ($7.95 or $11.95 per image)
  - Shutterstock, http://www.shutterstock.com (Price varies)
  - Deposit Photos, http://www.depositphotos.com (Price varies)
- **Cover Design Software**
  - Gimp (free), http://www.gimp.com
  - Paint (generally free on Windows machines), http://windows.microsoft.com/en-us/windows7/products/features/paint
  - Adobe PhotoShop (now, only available with a subscription; $9.99 per month)
  - Paint.NET - Free, http://www.getpaint.net/

Author Web Presence:
- Create Your Own Website (the three sites below will host your content free, and you can pay a nominal annual fee [$12] for your own domain name, such as www.myname.com)
  - Wordpress, http://www.wordpress.com
  - Google Sites, https://sites.google.com/
  - Blogger, https://www.blogger.com

- Goodreads Author Page, https://www.goodreads.com/author/program
- Author Central Author Page, https://authorcentral.amazon.com/

Review Sites
- Big Al's Books and Pals, http://booksandpals.blogspot.com/p/submitting-book-for-review.html
- BestChicklit.com, http://bestchicklit.com/?page_id=2044
- Rabid Readers, http://www.rabidreaders.com/about-us/
- Chuckles Book Cave, http://chucklesbookcave.blogspot.co.uk/
- The IndieView aggregate list, http://www.theindieview.com/indie-reviewers/
- Indie Book Reviewer aggregate list, https://indiebookreviewer.wordpress.com/

Advertising Sites
- BookBub, https://www.bookbub.com/home
- eReaders News Today, http://ereadernewstoday.com
- Pixel of Ink (currently closed to new ads), http://www.pixelofink.com/
- Kindle Books and Tips, http://fkbt.com/
- BookSends, http://booksends.com/
- BKnights Fiverr, https://www.fiverr.com/bknights
- Choosy Bookworm, http://choosybookworm.com
- Fussy Librarian, http://www.thefussylibrarian.com
- HotZippy, http://hotzippy.net/feature-your-book.html
- ReadCheaply.com, http://readcheaply.com/
- PeopleReads, http://www.peoplereads.com/
- EBookSoda, http://www.ebooksoda.com/
- Booktastik, http://booktastik.com/
- Read Freely, http://www.readfree.ly/submityourfreebook/

Blogs & Forums:
- **The Passive Voice,** http://www.thepassivevoice.com
- **The Writer's Café,** http://www.kboards.com/index.php?board=60.0
- **David Gaughran blog,** http://davidgaughran.wordpress.

com/
- **Indies Unlimited blog,** http://www.indiesunlimited.com
- **Kristen Lamb Blog,** http://warriorwriters.wordpress.com
- **Joe Konrath:** http://jakonrath.blogspot.com/
- **Kristine Kathryn Rusch,** http://kriswrites.com/business-rusch-publishing-articles/#sthash.N0nhqQHP.t21yODDq.dpbs
- **Writer Beware Blog** (warnings about scam publishers), http://accrispin.blogspot.com/
- **Preditors and Editors,** http://www.pred-ed.com
- **Dear Rich** (intellectual property law), http://dearrichblog.blogspot.com/

APPENDIX C: ACRONYM CHEAT SHEET/GLOSSARY

There are a fair number of acronyms bandied about in self-publishing. Even though all the acronyms are explained in the book, it's easy to forget some if you don't use them a lot. Here's a quick cheat sheet of all the acronyms and publishing terms that popped up in the book.

Acronyms
Epub — The ebook file type used for most other ereaders beside Kindle

Mobi. — The ebook file type used for Kindle

PDF — Portal Document Format. A computer file type read by most ereaders

D2D — Draft 2 Digital

KDP — Kindle Direct Publishing

KDP Select — The KDP program that requires your book be exclusive to Amazon

POD — Print on Demand

R4R — Read for Review

ARC — Advanced Review Copy

SEO — Search Engine Optimization

TBR — To be Read

Glossary
Beta Readers — People who read your book before it's published and offer feedback

Tagline — A pithy, tantalizing sentence to describe your book

APPENDIX D: ARTICLES

These articles discuss writing, marketing and other issues self-published authors might face. Most of these articles first appeared on Indies Unlimited. I've included the text and provided a link to the original article, as some of the tutorials included images on the original site where they were published.

Fitting a Prequel into Your Series
Posted on August 25, 2014 by RJ Crayton

George Lucas has done many wonderful things for the world (*Star Wars, American Graffiti, Star Wars, Indiana Jones, Star Wars*), but one of the most fun is his popularization of the term "prequel." According to Wikipedia (that hub of fan information that hasn't necessarily been vetted), the term appeared sometime in 1956, but wasn't popularized until Lucas announced he was doing a "prequel" to his Star Wars trilogy that would give backstory of Darth Vader.

By definition, a prequel is a sequel. It comes after the original work was written. However, it's the backstory component that leads up to how the main characters got to be who they are.

While I love George's popularization of the prequel, I'm not that happy with one other thing he popularized: re-numbering the series to make it seem as if the prequel should be read/watched first. There are many things I loved about *Star Wars: Episode I*, but I'm not sure I would have sat through that much Jar Jar had I not watched the now renamed *Star Wars Episodes IV*, V (OMG, Darth Vader is Luke's father!), and VI.

I was visiting an online writers forum the other day, and someone mentioned that they had a trilogy where the first book they wrote in the series (we'll call it book one) was perma-free. The author had written a prequel to the series and was considering making the prequel perma-free, because, under the author's logic, that prequel would now be book one.

But that's just the thing. The prequel is not book one. The prequel is book four. The prequel doesn't have the same payoff, the same inside jokes, or even the same love and adoration if you read it first. Reading the prequel first leaves readers at a disadvantage. They don't come at it with the same reactions, or the same sense of anticipation.

With rare exception, I think all books should be labeled in the order they were published. Even if the events of the fourth book published occurred before the events of the first book published, it's hard to get the same payoff if the book written fourth is read first. The writer knows the characters inside and out by book four and is going to make references and inside jokes based on what's happened in previous iterations. If the author is writing it in that order, and readers of the series have experienced it in that order, why would we label it in anything but that order?

Want an example of when re-numbering a series doesn't work? The *Chronicles of Narnia* by CS Lewis. When I first read these books as a youngster, I read them in the order they were published. Back then, when you bought a set of the books, they were numbered (based on publication date). I went to get the *Chronicles* for my children and guess what? They are now numbered chronologically, based on the events in the book.

The book that started it all, *The Lion, the Witch, and the Wardrobe*, is now book two in the series. Book one is *The Magician's Nephew* (which was published sixth). *The Magician's Nephew* has wonderful inside jokes for anyone who's read the rest of the series, but all of them will fall flat if you read this book first. I truly adored those books when I first read them, but I wonder if *The Magician's Nephew* would capture enough people's fancy that they'd want to go on to Wardrobe, if they start with it. *The Magician's Nephew* is not a bad book, but I don't know that it introduces you to the magic of Narnia with the same wonder you got when Lucy tumbled through the wardrobe and onto a snowy street beneath that lamp post. (By the way, check out these Amazon reviews of *The Chronicles of Narnia* series. The reviews focus mostly on the order in which the books are numbered, rather than the content.)

Remember folks, a prequel is, at its core, a sequel. Just like any other sequel, its number should correspond to the order you think it should be read in. I've just started a prequel to my *Life First* series, and I know exactly what it will be numbered: Book Four.

http://www.indiesunlimited.com/2014/08/25/fitting-a-prequel-into-your-series/

Tips on Creating a Story Bible
Posted on March 24, 2014 by RJ Crayton

So, you're editing the last part of your novel and mention a character's sister named Annie. Or was it Annabeth? Or did you give in to that wild idea of changing the sister's name to Rasheeda? You can't remember, because you only mentioned the sister once — in chapter three. What do you do now? You could do a search for all three names. Or you could turn to your story bible.

What's a story bible? Like the persistent bestseller it's named after, the story bible is a guide book of sorts. It's a compilation of all the crucial facts about your book. It lays out character backgrounds, story setting details, pertinent acronyms, and everything else you need to know in one easy-to-find place. This is very useful when editing. And it's downright essential if you're writing a sequel, either a series or serial, as Stephen Hise discussed [40]not long ago.

A story bible sounds cool, right? How do you get one? Well, you have to create it yourself. What you put in it is up to you, and how detailed you make it is up to you. These are the basics to include: characters, locations, and world-specific stuff you made up.

Before we go deeper, I'll just note that it's easiest to create your story bible either upfront or as you go along, depending on how you write. If you're a plotter, filling in the character information for your story bible may help you in plotting. If you're a pantser, where you just write what comes to mind, take a few minutes at the end of your writing session (or beginning of next) to record any pertinent details that emerged during the writing session. Plotters should do the writing day update too, as even plotters come up with new details as they write. If you're already done with your novel, it's not too late for a story bible. Just go back through your novel and create entries based on the guidelines below.

Now, back to those three basic items your story bible should include. With characters, you want to include their name, age, and physical descriptions — including eye and hair color as well as build (fat, lean, pudgy, femme-fatale curvy). In physical descriptions, you can include any scars, or other identifying marks. Beyond the physical, you want background info on where they're from, family members, best

---

[40] Stephen Hise article, http://www.indiesunlimited.com/2014/03/07/series-vs-serials/

friends, level of education, and even names of schools they've attended, or companies they've worked for if those details are in your book. You can go deeper and give information that's not in the book if you want to, but that's not a requirement. You'll appreciate that deeper info later, if you're writing a series or serialized novel. However, as the goal of a story bible is to help maintain consistency; the most important things to include are things that are in the novel.

The second thing to include in your story bible is what I call location info. If there are certain places your characters visit repeatedly, you should give them an entry in your story bible so the details of the place stay the same. If your characters hang out in a coffee shop, it shouldn't suddenly have an upstairs in book four, when it's described as a single story building in book one.

Finally, you'll want to include anything you created as part of your story's world. To avoid legal entanglements (possible libel/intellectual property lawsuits), many fiction writers create some imaginary businesses or acronyms. If you write science fiction or fantasy, you're probably going to have a fair amount of things you made up to world build. Those should go in the story bible. This would include things like acronyms, business names, creatures, or special technology. For example, my characters have LMS chips (life monitoring system) in their arms, so it's in my story bible.

A story bible is meant to be a reference guide for you (or your editor) while you're editing or writing, so it doesn't have to include every detail of your book. But it should include information necessary for you to be consistent. It would be nice to say that the story bible should only include things you're going to mention a lot, but chances are, if you mention something a lot, you'll remember the detail. Story bibles help you with the things you're unlikely to remember. It will keep characters from having brown eyes on page eight and hazel eyes on page 208 (or for eBooks, location 623 vs location 3244). You'll also avoid name changes similar to the ones I mentioned in the opener.

So, do you have a story bible? Would anyone like to share the biggest gaffe they almost made before checking the facts?

http://www.indiesunlimited.com/2014/03/24/tips-on-creating-a-story-bible/

Do Book Posts in Facebook Groups Work as Marketing?
Posted on December 22, 2014 by RJ Crayton

I am a heavy user of Facebook, personally. I belong to a lot of writer groups, and several groups that allow book promotion (you post a spiffy description and link to your book — typically the Amazon link). Several authors I've encountered have expressed great disdain at these promo groups, saying they're a waste of time and filled with other authors posting promos, not real readers. The critics also argue that posting on these sites just clutters your news feed, showing your friends your crappy, lazy marketing efforts.

However, my newsfeed has been cluttered by several authors doing this, and to me, it seemed crazy that people would continue to do something that is completely ineffective. So, being the evidence monger that I am, I decided to conduct an experiment to see if these Facebook marketing posts actually work. My conclusion — sorry, Charlie, I'm gonna make you read to the end to find out. Or maybe I'll tell you at some point before the end so you have to keep reading and can't just skip to the bottom (I'm laughing maniacally right now).

To start my experiment, I identified 16 Facebook groups that allow you to post a promo for your book (this is super important; DO NOT post promos in groups that don't allow it!). Some people post several posts to different groups all at the same time, and that really does clutter the newsfeed (you see 10 duplicate posts in a row from the person). Not wanting to do that, I decided to post to one group each day. That way I could determine if that particular post had an effect on sales. Then, I set up a spreadsheet and identified the group I posted in, the date I posted, the time I posted, the promo language I posted, whether the group was open or closed, and then finally the result.

A quick note about two of the data points I recorded. I included whether the group was open or closed because posts to closed groups do not show up in your newsfeed (unless your friend also belongs to that group). My thinking was that if I found any closed groups that got decent results, I would know I could post there more often without cluttering my newsfeed. Second, in the "result" column, I actually ended up recording two pieces of data, so I probably should've broken this into two data points. The two data points I recorded in the column were the number of sales I had at the time I made the post, followed by the number of sales that appeared within four hours of the post (on my KDP dashboard).

Now, I am not a scientist, so this experiment had too many variables for the results to be of much long-standing value to the community of writers. But, that wasn't my goal. My goal was to try to see what things worked, if anything. So, I did vary the times of day I posted, to see if I noticed a trend that I got better results posting at 3 pm instead of 10 pm, or something like that. However, to be more scientific, you'd probably want to do this longer, keeping the time element consistent for several weeks, then changing it and posting at the new time for several weeks. I decided to do no advertising whatsoever for my books during this period (other than the Facebook posts). I did continue my regular blogging schedule (Indies Unlimited and my personal blog), but didn't add any guest posts. I conducted my experiment between June 8 and July 17.

I posted to the following groups:

1. ebooksnpromo
   https://www.facebook.com/groups/eBooksBooksPromo/
2. BOOKS BOOKS N MORE BOOKS
   https://www.facebook.com/groups/320356974732142/
3. Authors, Reviewers, & Book Lovers/
   https://www.facebook.com/groups/BooksLuvers/
4. BOOK PLACE
   https://www.facebook.com/groups/bookplace/
5. ALL ABOUT BOOKS
   https://www.facebook.com/groups/9476163038/
6. NOVELSPOT
   https://www.facebook.com/groups/NovelspotRecommends books/
7. BOOKS GONE VIRAL
   https://www.facebook.com/groups/booksgoneviral/
8. INDIE AUTHOR GROUP
   https://www.facebook.com/groups/571135069563269/
9. PASSION for BOOKS
   https://www.facebook.com/groups/passionforbooks/
10. BOOK PROMOTIONS
    https://www.facebook.com/groups/623206594363552/
11. Kindel Mojo

https://www.facebook.com/groups/kindlemojo/
12. ONLINE BOOK PUBLICITY GROUP
    https://www.facebook.com/groups/online.book.publicity/
13. BOOKS https://www.facebook.com/groups/books45/
14. KINDLE GOODREADS
    https://www.facebook.com/groups/kindle.goodreads/
15. PROMOTE YOUR BOOK
    https://www.facebook.com/groups/201856639887358/
16. 2 FRIENDS PROMOTE YOUR BOOK WITH US (UK based) (https://www.facebook.com/groups/2friends promatewithauthors/

What I found was that results were inconsistent. Some days I got sales after a post, other days I didn't. Some days I got a sale following a post, but not a sale for the book I posted about. About midway through I hypothesized I was doing better by posting in larger groups (those with 10,000 or more members), but when I went back and looked at the data over the course of the whole experiment, that didn't appear to hold true. At one point, it seemed that posting after 11 pm worked well (are those late night infomercial watchers book buyers too?), so I tried doing posts mainly after 11 for a while and that didn't seem to produce results.

I gave up on my Facebook posting in July because I was posting consistently each day and not seeing sales as a result. Obviously, it wasn't arduous to copy and paste a post, but I was trying to finish a book and I just didn't have time to record the data for something that wasn't netting a lot of reward.

Do the posts work? Sometimes. The problem is I saw no consistency in it. However, to be fair, because this wasn't a true scientific experiment, I can't say these posts can't be used effectively in marketing. There were tons of variables at play. It could just be that I have a sucky blurb, and people with better blurbs do better. Or maybe readers who belong to these groups prefer romance or Christian fiction or zombies (and the book I was posting about was none of those genres). Also, I did these posts while my book was priced $2.99. Anecdotally speaking, in the past I've posted when my book was discounted to 99 cents and seen what appeared to be a related sale or two. However, my mini experiment didn't look at the impact a discount has on effectiveness of these posts (which may be crucial).

If you're interested in the effectiveness of posting in these groups, I'd definitely suggest you run your own experiment and see if you find the posting worth your time or not.

http://www.indiesunlimited.com/2014/12/22/do-book-posts-in-facebook-groups-work-as-marketing/

Create an Author Holiday Card to Help Connect with Readers
Posted on November 24, 2014 by RJ Crayton

If you're the type of person who sends a spiffy holiday card and newsletter to your family and friends, you may be the kind of author who wants to do the same to your fans.

As a person, I am definitely all-in on the holiday card and catching-up newsletter. We do a picture (in a costume of some sort), a website, and a brief summary of the excitement of the year. Lots of fun for family and friends who want to catch up.

So, how do you translate this to your author persona? Simple. Do the same thing, only author-related and send it to your newsletter subscribers. It's a chance for you to connect with fans in a way that they normally connect with friends and family. Therefore, we want it to be similar to what we'd send to friends and family.

First up is a picture — go for fun, but appropriate as an author. It could be you in a Santa hat. You holding a holiday ornament. You spinning a dreidel. Fun, festive, and with a hint of decorum (one year, I put my children in giant gift bags for our holiday card, but that probably is a bit iffy in the author decorum department). You could also use your most recent book for an image if you don't want to be in the image. Take a picture of the book peeking out of a stocking or nestled in a wreath.

Next up, you'll want a holiday greeting of some sort. Offer the kind of greeting you feel comfortable giving. Happy Holidays covers Hanukkah, Christmas, and Kwanzaa, and is appropriate if you're sending in early December. In recent years, there has been backlash against "Happy Holidays" at times, with some people feeling it's a move to shun Christmas. Season's Greetings is more neutral. Or go with Merry Christmas if you like it and that's the sentiment you want to offer.

Next up, give a short message about your year in review. Just a quick wrap up of any highlights. If you've published any books, won any awards, or completed any other projects, mention them. While readers may enjoy your work, they're busy people and may have missed your mailing about the new book; or saw the mailing, but forgot to buy the book. It's a great reminder for people who've been subscribers to your list all year. For those new to the list, it's also a great chance for them to get an overview.

Also, include anything new for the month of December. If you're one of those people who likes to release a Christmas-themed book or just have a new book that happens to be publishing in December, this is a great place to mention it. Also, if you're having any holiday sales, include the dates and titles that will be on sale.

Finally, give your readers a holiday gift of some sort. It can be a coupon code for a retail site, a favorite holiday recipe you share with them, or even a short story you're posting for free. Or all of the above or something else entirely. Everyone loves free around the holidays, so why not give it to them?

For the holiday card newsletter, try to keep it short, so readers can quickly get to the end, but also get plenty of info. If you're including a free gift, be sure your email subject line indicates that (as in, "Holiday Greetings Plus a Free Gift"). On days when I open my inbox to 200 messages, I've been ready to trash unopened emails I've subscribed to, but then I see the word "free" and the cheapskate — wait, I mean frugalista — in me has to open it. In addition to sending it to current subscribers, you can also post the holiday card on your author website along with a newsletter sign-up form at the bottom. This might net you an additional sign up or two from the drop-in reader.

http://www.indiesunlimited.com/2014/11/24/create-an-author-holiday-card-to-help-connect-with-readers/

Authors Can Share Words as Images to Widen Reach
Posted on October 27, 2014 by RJ Crayton

You've probably seen them. You may even have shared them: an image that contains a really cool quote.

Last month, Jim Devitt told us that images get more interaction than text, so turning text from your novel into an image is a great way to increase reach, while getting out word about your book. Image quotes also allow authors to interact on image-based social media (like Pinterest) with something other than their book covers.

If you think image quotes are something you'd like to try, here is the skinny on what you need to know to make it work.

Can Any Author Do This? Yep. Image quotes are great for both fiction and nonfiction authors. It may be most effective for nonfiction books, as they can include useful tips that people want to share, pass on, and read more about (I've seen a lot of self-help tidbits as quotes). However, image quotes are also a good way to showcase fiction, so long as you have good content (see next point).

Picking a Quote — This is the hardest and most important part of the process. (The Evil Mastermind wrote about choosing a book excerpt — much of the same logic applies here.) You need to find a quote from your book that is tantalizing, fun, or intriguing enough that it will catch people's attention, and they'll want to find out more and/or share it with others. With fiction, the quote can be either narrative or a quote from a character. For example, this would be a great image quote: "Tact is the ability to tell someone to go to hell in such a way that they look forward to the trip." This quote, however, is attributed to Winston Churchill (while I love the quote, I still have no idea how to accomplish it; I guess I lack tact). My point is, if your characters have great, spitfire sayings/advice, showcase it. Anything that's eye-catching (and appropriate for general audiences; no porn scenes, please) will work. If it's nonfiction, pointers or tips always make great quotes. If you're looking for examples of quote content, check out our own Big Al's Facebook Page.

Quote Length — It can't be too long. People don't want to read a novel as a single image. They want pithy, newsbyte-sized pieces. Go for fewer than 35 words. Before posting, look at the image quote to see if it's easily legible. Does it seem too dense or the text too tiny? If so, cut down the quote or get a better one. In the span of a novel, it can be hard to find short quotes that make sense without reading the surrounding text. However, it's worth doing if you're going to make an image quote. (If you can tweet a quote, you can manage this.) If you do a lot of cutting to get your quote to fit, be sure to run it by someone who hasn't read the book to make sure the reduced quote makes sense (sometimes we can be oblivious that we've cut necessary context).

Take Credit — With Pinterest, Facebook, Instagram, etc., once an image gets shared, it's often difficult to figure out where it originated. So, it's important thing to tag your image. I'm speaking of tagging in a graffiti sense, not a keyword sense. You need to put your author information somewhere on the image. The quote will be the main text, but somewhere in the periphery, include your URL or author name. Most people aren't going to go track down your site based on the quote, but occasionally someone will. They'll like the quote so much they'll want more and be prepared to type in your URL or Google search your author name. But they can't do that if you don't provide them with a starting point. A URL is probably the best way to tag your image, so long as the URL isn't super long. Remember, tagging the image with your URL is so people can find you — the originator of the quote — when they read it on a site that has nothing to do with you (and that's a good thing, because that means your quote has been shared a lot).

Design — Most authors are not graphic designers. For quotes, you don't have to be. However, you do have to use some common sense. Make the font big enough that people can read it. Don't use hard-to-read fonts. San serifs are often easier to read than serif fonts. If you choose a dark background (brown, navy blue, maroon), don't use black text. Instead, pick a light color, such as white or yellow, so there's enough contrast that it can be read easily. Most quotes appear on a background that is a single color or something subdued, so the text is the most prominent visual. As that's what seems to be working for a lot of people, I would recommend following that model. When you introduce things like clouds, mountains, or your favorite bird, you run the risk of it interfering with text legibility. You might be able to use your book cover or elements of it a background, but remember that text legibility is more important than the background. If you have design experience, use it, and do what makes sense. If, like me, you don't have design experience, then keep it simple. If you're looking for some examples of various image quote designs, check out the Timeless Literary Quotes Pinterest Page.

Linking — Let's say someone is so enamored of the quote, they want to buy the book right that second. Well, you can provide a buy link using the method that makes sense for the social network you're using to share the image. For example, Pinterest offers a description area. You might restate the quote, add a line of description about the book the quote is from and then include the buy link. On Facebook, the picture is going to show up as your status when you post it, so you may want to provide a more traditional status update, and provide the link in the photo caption. You can also take a hands-off approach and provide no link at all or just a link to the URL you tagged your image with (rather than a specific retailer's buy link).

Image quotes are fairly easy to create, but we've post a how-to tutorial[41] showing step-by-step (with screenshots) how to make one using Google Drive, which is free online software available to anyone with a Gmail account.

http://www.indiesunlimited.com/2014/10/27/authors-can-share-words-as-images-to-widen-reach/

---

[41] Tutorial, http://indiesunlimited.com/2014/10/28/tutorial-how-to-create-image-quotes/

A website has emerged with the goal of introducing readers to books through the power of excerpt.

Posted on September 22, 2014 by RJ Crayton

Microcerpt[42], which is free to authors and readers, allows authors to post short excerpts (Microcerpts) from their books onto the site. Readers can browse the excerpts, and if they're tantalized by one, buy the book.

As Lynne Cantwell reminded us in her post on effective frequency, it's important to be seen in multiple places, so I joined Microcerpt in March of this year. I was going to write about it earlier, but they revamped their platform in mid-July, so I wanted to wait until that passed to see if there were any new features to discuss.

I found it fairly easy to set up a Microcerpt excerpt. To do so, you just need to create a free account. Then, you'll need to have the excerpt you want in a place that's easy for you to copy and paste from. You may also want to include an image with your Microcerpt — generally the book cover, but you can use something different if you want.

Microcerpts are limited to 1,000 words, so pick a section of text that is intriguing and exciting within that word count. (The Evil Mastermind wrote a post about choosing an effective excerpt here.) A new feature that was added in the site revamp is the ability to put a link at the bottom of your Microcerpt to your book on Amazon. When I first signed up, that was not a choice, but it was there when I added my latest Microcerpt.

You can add as many Microcerpts as you want, but they have to have different titles. So, if you wanted multiple Microcerpts from one book, you'd need to differentiate them. This can be done with a simple word or two. For example, you can use "Book Name — Excerpt One," and then title the next one "Book Name — Excerpt Two." However, since this is a marketing tool, you may want to have a little more fun with it. I titled one of my excerpts Life First — Deadly Virus[43] and the other Life First — Marked.

Once you've finished filling out the info form to create the Microcerpt, including keywords so searchers can find your work, you'll click "Submit Post." When you do this, all your information disappears so

---

[42] Microcerpt home page, http://microcerpt.com/

[43] Deadly Virus Microcerpt. http://microcerpt.com/rjcrayton/blog/2014/03/deadly-virus/

you see a blank version of every field you just filled out. This is initially disconcerting, but don't worry. Your post did not disappear into the ether. Scroll to the bottom of the page, and you'll see a little green box with the words, "You can check your post here." Click the hyperlinked "here" and you'll see your Microcerpt. You can also see it from the navigation menu on the right side of the page (under my Microcerpts).

Microcerpt posts excerpts to its social networks, but free accounts get a maximum of one posting per week (though it's not guaranteed), no matter how often/many Microcerpts the account user posts. You can pay a fee to get additional social networking posts, prominent positioning on the home page, or other services. The site has roughly 11,000 Facebook fans and 10,000 Twitter followers.

In addition to the exposure to potential readers, Microcerpt also has interactive forums, such as "Authors Helping Authors," "Book Reviews & Authors," and "Book Marketing Support Group." While I uploaded my first Microcerpt a few months back and receive a digest of the forum posts, I haven't gotten a good sense of how many readers actively participate on the site or view the excerpts. However, because it's free exposure, I don't see any downside to posting an excerpt on the site.

http://www.indiesunlimited.com/2014/09/22/microcerpt-exploits-power-of-the-excerpt/

Plugins Every Author Can Use
Posted on July 28, 2014 by RJ Crayton

As authors, it's important for us to have a website or blog devoted to our work. A common and easy way to do this is to use WordPress or Google (via Blogger or Google Sites). Neither method requires HTML knowledge, so they're easy to use and manage. While these sites are pretty basic, we authors can use plugins (for WordPress) or widgets (Blogger) to add fancy features that would normally require us to know all sorts of programming languages (XML, HTML, JAVA) if we had to create them on our own.

So, today I'm offering up some cool plugins/widgets all authors should consider for their sites.

Social/Subscribe bar — These are bars that run across the top of a website (on every page) that let viewers subscribe to your mailing list or follow you on social media. I use Viper Bar[44] on my own site, and love it. Users can subscribe to my mailing list or follow me on Facebook, Twitter, Google+, Tumblr, and/or Pinterest. Viper Bar is nice in that it's easy to set up for mailing lists. However, if you want to add social sharing, you've got to code that yourself. I did. Because I'm so awesome, I'm uploading the exact code I used[45] and images (logos are public domain) so you can crib it if you want (don't forget to substitute your own URLs in the indicated spots). Hello Bar[46] is also a good option. The company used to charge for each click over 25 (so, in an odd way, it was good if you had to pay). However, I checked them out recently, and there's no fee. These are both great options, and very helpful. Our social media guru Jim Devitt has told us often that a subscriber list is key[47] in your marketing, so having the ability for visitors to see that option whenever they visit your site is great. Viper Bar works with WordPress. Hello Bar works with any website or blog.

Social Sharing Buttons — If you have great content on your blog,

---

[44] Viper Bar, http://www.viperchill.com/viperbar/
[45] Link to code: http://rjcrayton.com/extras/viperbar_iu.html
[46] Hello Bar, https://www.hellobar.com/
[47] Jim Devitt on subscriber lists, http://www.indiesunlim-ited.com/2014/02/10/fifteen-ways-to-grow-your-email-list/

you want people who visit your website to share it. So, add social sharing buttons to the bottom of your blog posts. Social sharing buttons are those little icons that, when clicked, let readers share your post on Twitter, Facebook, Pinterest, etc. There are tons of social sharing button plugins out there. I like Share-a-Holic[48]. It has large prominent buttons that display above or below post and tell readers how many times the post has been shared via each network. Another good one is Social Sharing Toolkit[49]. With both of these, they give you a spot to add your Twitter username. Do this. That way, when people Tweet from your website, you'll be tagged in the tweet. If you don't do it, the companies actually tag themselves in the post (shared via @). Social Sharing Toolkit is for WordPress. Share-a-Holic works for any site.

Related Content — I've read a few articles noting that it's important to keep people at your site as long as possible. If someone stumbles upon your blog post, you don't want them to read it and leave. You want them to check out the rest of the site and get more exposure to you and your work. One way to keep people on your site is with a Related Content feature. What good plugins do is comb through your blog for related posts that might interest the reader of the current post. It displays three or four related articles at the bottom of the post, so that rather than leave your site, the reader goes, "Oooooooh! That looks interesting," and clicks the link. Ideally, related content buttons would leave your readers in fear of wetting their pants because they don't want to tear themselves away from your site. Share-a-Holic has a related content feature as part of its plugin. I used it and found it wasn't bringing up related content. One web critique I read about the service said the "related content" feature was new and it was expected to improve. I wish them luck with that, but I moved on and got nRelate, which I love. The related content has all been relevant, and when I look at my website stats, I'm seeing people randomly viewing older articles which appear to have been suggested as related. All related content plugins use your keywords, categories and tags to help determine which content is related, so be sure to add keywords and tags to all your blog posts (if you don't the algorithms will have more trouble figuring out which content is related). There are a fair number of related content plugins; this guy offers his thoughts on the

---

[48] Share-a-Holic, https://shareaholic.com/
[49] Social Sharing Toolkit, https://wordpress.org/plugins/social-sharing-toolkit/

five best. **[NOTE: Since the writing of this post, nRelate stopped doing related content for the public. The company suggest people who want that service try the company Limk[50].]**

So those were the essentials. There are two optional plugins I thought I'd include. They're fun, but not musts.

Fancier Author Box[51] — This is an optional plugin for WordPress users. It just puts abbreviated bio information at the bottom of each blog post. You could just type the info at the bottom of each post, but this plugin eliminates that extra step of doing it manually. I use it and like it. For a fee, you can upgrade to Fanciest Author Box.

Image book buy links — On your book's page, instead of writing Buy at Amazon or Buy at Barnes and Noble and making it a hypertext link, what if you had an image of all the stores' logos neatly lined up with the images serving as links? I tried doing this with html and it was a pain in the you know where. Particularly hard was getting the image sizes right and lining everything up by hand-coding it (this may be a function of my limited HTML knowledge). So, I looked it up and there are plugins that say they will do this for you. These are the three I found: Buy This Book[52], Totally Booked[53], and My Book Table[54]. Unfortunately, after trying them out, I wasn't pleased with any of them. One looked funky and I couldn't get the other two to work with my existing site. If you're building your site from scratch, give any of these guys a try, as they seemed geared toward sites that didn't already have book pages. If your site's already built, this may be a frustrating process that isn't worth it (based on my own experience and the reviews on the product pages). Do read the reviews before trying any of these, as one plugin actually deleted my book page (as in, it was gone forever). It didn't matter because a one-star review warned of this and I'd saved a copy of the original; I just had to re-upload it. But if I hadn't read the reviews, I'd have been quite upset. If you know of a better plugin to

---

[50] Limk, https://limk.com/

[51] Fancier Author Box, https://wordpress.org/plugins/fancier-author-box/

[52] Buy This Book, https://wordpress.org/plugins/buy-this-book/

[53] Totally Booked, https://wordpress.org/support/view/plugin-reviews/totally-booked

[54] My Book Table, https://wordpress.org/plugins/mybooktable/

do this, leave a comment, as I'd still be interested in one that works seamlessly with an existing site.

So, I think I've covered the basics. Any plugin you think I've missed that you absolutely love? Or one I've mentioned that you're now going to try?

http://www.indiesunlimited.com/2014/07/28/plugins-every-author-can-use/

Creating a Short Story Collection
Posted on June 23, 2014 by RJ Crayton

Many authors write the occasional short story, but because of their length, may not want to sell them as a single item.

A short story collection is a great way to release some shorts with a word count that makes the price reasonable.

Creating a short story collection is a little different from creating a traditional novel, so here are a few things to consider:

• **Collection theme.** It's good to have a general theme for the collection. That helps ground readers in what they're getting and solidifies the reason the stories are together. A tagline that expresses the gist of your theme can also help quickly sum up the collection in potential readers' minds. For example, if your collection theme is mysteries, you could use a tagline like, "Mysteries to keep you up all night." If the theme is cozy mysteries, maybe you use something like, "Cozy up for a night of intrigue."

• **Introductions & TOCs.** An introduction is often appropriate for collections. It only has to be about a paragraph and should let the reader know the general theme of the collection. While some people don't believe a table of contents is necessary in novels, I think a short story collection should have one. TOCs let readers know all the stories in the collection. They also allow readers to easily pick a story they want to start with. If that's the way they like to read collections, they should easily be able to get to the story they want to read first.

• **Story order.** While this may seem insignificant, story order does matter. You want to lead with one of your strongest stories, one that readers will devour so quickly they'll want to keep reading all the rest. Of course, all the titles in the collection should be good, but it's important to start strong. In looking at short story collections for sale on Amazon, many collections' one-star reviews indicated the first story the reviewer read was poor. On one collection I saw, a four-star reviewer implored others to give the collection a chance because it starts off weakly. That's not what any author wants. Saving the best for last doesn't work in books, because readers tend not to wait that long. (I know I mentioned skippers earlier, but for every person who likes to skip around, there's another who likes to start at the beginning and move to the end.)

• **Book Description.** Because it's a collection of stories, you can't write the typical linear narrative you would craft for a novel description. Short story collection descriptions vary in method, but the first thing you'll want to do is start with your theme. This is where your tagline can come in handy. Then, provide a few sentences that describe some of the tales in the collection. If you have 25 stories, you can't describe them all. Pick a few. Some collections list the title of all the stories in the bottom part of the product description (mainly when there are multiple authors); others choose to leave that information to the book's Table of Contents.

- **Cover.** As always, check to see what other covers look like for your genre. Romance collections look different from horror. People have varying opinions on this, but I think it's important to say it's a short story collection on the cover. Readers should look at the description, but sometimes they don't. It's best to avoid confusion with a little clarity on the cover.

- **Promoting Your Other Work.** One thing marketers suggest is to promote your other work at the end of your book. One way is to put an excerpt from another novel at the end of the newest work. With short story collections, you have to make an extra assessment before deciding if and how much of an excerpt to provide. If the short story collection is very short, you'll probably want to include as minimal an excerpt as possible or no excerpt. While writers like to promote the excerpt as "bonus material," readers sometimes feel cheated if half the length of the eBook is an excerpt from another work. The longer your collection is, the more comfortable you can feel adding a short opening chapter from one of your other novels at the end. The shorter your collection, the more you may want to think about it.

Those were the major things to look out for when dealing with short story collections.

http://www.indiesunlimited.com/2014/06/23/creating-a-short-story-collection/

Book Festival Experts Offer Advice on Building Author Platform
Posted on March 31, 2014 by RJ Crayton

So, once you've published a book, platform building and marketing strategies are the next things to tackle on the to-do list. At the Virginia Festival of the Book, this past March 23rd, several authors and experts discussed the best ways to build platform and market books.

First up, we'll discuss platform building. Platform is more or less all the things that make up your author persona. It includes everything from social media to your work to your general reputation in the author world. Platform building is one of the strongest parts of your marketing strategy, but it's also the most difficult, the experts said.

"Your platform is part of your job as a writer," said Bethanne Patrick, author of An Uncommon History of Common Things who built a large following (186k) tweeting as @thebookmaven. "Many of us would rather be writing and researching. But it is not optional. It is something that has to be done."

Many authors are especially wary of social media, viewing it as a huge time-suck. So, when you're too busy, what thing do you give up? Gigi Amateau had a humorous response: "The thing you stop doing is the laundry. You go to Target and buy about six weeks of underpants," she joked.

Amateau, author of numerous children's books, then offered some serious advice. "Author platform is the inverted pyramid," she said. "The biggest part of the platform is the books. It is where I'm the most authentic, vulnerable, and risk-taking. That's the biggest part of my platform. The second priority for me is engaging with my community in person. The third little piece is where I would put online. I think there are ways, even as introverts, that you can fall in love with that."

Jane Friedman, former Writers Digest publisher who now teaches digital publishing at the University of Virginia, agreed. "Platform grows out of your body of work. That's where it all starts and ends," Friedman said. "The hope is it grows organically out of that. This isn't like drawing a line from point A to point B. There is a lot of serendipity involved. The most important thing is consistency and seeing your efforts pay off. You're not going to go home tonight and nail your platform and then not have to do it anymore."

Denise Kiernan, author of the nonfiction book Girls of the Atomic

City, expressed similar sentiments. "People are a little too anxious to look for a magic bullet — like if I get 500,000 Twitter followers, it will be OK," Kiernan said.

Most panelists agreed authors shouldn't try to force social media, saying doing so would make it appear, well, forced. "Just be sure it's something you like to do," Kiernan said. "Some people like Facebook better than Twitter. Some people like to go on blog tours and write for them because they like that network. Experiment and go with what you enjoy most."

Keeping that in mind, Friedman said that platform builds over time as authors put out more work. "An author's long-term career is rarely tied to a single publisher or a single book. Your platform or career should outlast that one single book or deal."

One audience member posed the question of whether an author should focus on trying to appeal to the broader market or go deep into a narrow pool of readers. "Coming from a publisher who was a niche publisher, I have seen the power of going deep," Friedman said. "Assuming you are going to be going back to that audience, the rewards grow with each passing book. It is easier to start narrow and then broaden your reach. There are things you can do to cast a wider net, but I would go after the true fans first."

Another thing authors should do — and sadly, it has to be said — is be nice. "No whining, no jealousy, or anything that is just bad personhood," said Sharyn Rosenblum, a vice president at William Morrow who spent many years as an in-house publicist. "Have a positive attitude and don't be cranky."

Maud Casey, a literary fiction author, agreed. "The lesson here is we're people. You're forging relationships with human beings," she said. "Bad personhood is not a good idea in general, and especially in within the publishing community. Be kind, be curious."

Part II will look at some specific marketing strategies recommended.

http://www.indiesunlimited.com/2014/04/07/experts-talk-marketing-strategies-at-virginia-book-festival/

Experts Talk Marketing Strategies at Virginia Book Festival
Posted on April 7, 2014 by RJ Crayton

At the Virginia Festival of the Book, this past March 23rd, several authors and experts talked about the best ways to build platform, as well as some specific marketing strategies. Last time we looked at platform building. Now, let's look at marketing.

First and foremost, when it comes to marketing, think about trying to reach your reader. This is something that indie authors can do particularly well. Jane Friedman, former Writers Digest publisher who now teaches digital publishing at the University of Virginia, noted that traditional publishers have failed in gathering information about readers. "They're selling to bookstores, so they don't have these great email lists or insights into the market," Friedman said. Authors can look more broadly at readers and try to reach them. Email is an especially effective way.

"Email has proven to be a really powerful tool," Friedman said. "Publishers don't have a lot of direct consumer data. They can't say to the people who bought the book before that a new book is out by that author. That's why it's important to have an email list. It is one of the most powerful investments an author can make in their career. It's like putting money in the bank, every time you get someone signing up." Jim DeVitt wrote a post about email newsletters[55] last month.

Friedman said she'd seen writers with email newsletter frequencies vary: annually, quarterly, bimonthly and monthly. She felt bimonthly or monthly worked best, and if you only go annually, your reader is likely to "forget they subscribed and mark you as spam."

In addition to email lists, Gigi Amateau, author of several children's books, says authors need to find their community of readers. "Every book intersects with its own community. Think about the story you've written and who might be interested in it," Amateau said, noting she went to a different audience from her norm with her book about horses. "Kids in 4-H are into them. It is a place where I can talk to people about it, and they're interested in it."

If there is an association or a group that might be affiliated with the

---

[55] Devitt post on email newsletters, http://www.indiesunlimited.com/2014/02/17/developing-the-perfect-author-newsletter

subject matter of your book, go there. Try to engage with that community and get word of your book out.

Author Maud Casey has a book is based on the story of a 19th century man who suffered numerous fugue states where he woke up places and couldn't remember how he got there. During research for this book, Casey heard about a scientist studying memory and has become involved in a community of neurologists who are now interested in and discussing her book.

Two conference speakers reminded people that getting journalists interested in publicizing your story is helpful. While it may sound like a daunting task, it is perfectly possible, says Denise Kiernan, author of the book Girls of the Atomic City.

"Think like a journalist," Kiernan said. "They are looking for you as much as you are looking for them. It's easy for you to think, I want to be in the magazine so I'm in a position of weakness. But as a journalist, you have to fill your newspaper, you have to fill that blog. The author has to ask, what does that person need? If you give them the angle they need, they are thrilled to publicize your book."

Kiernan appeared on the Daily Show with Jon Stewart to talk about her book. She readily admits it was a combination of pitching and luck. Her pitch ended up being routed to a producer who liked the angle, and that producer pitched it to Stewart, who read the book and liked it. If either the producer or Stewart hadn't liked it, the appearance wouldn't have happened. But, you'll never find out, Kiernan notes, if you don't make the pitch.

Sharyn Rosenblum, a vice president at William Morrow who spent many years as an in-house publicist, said one thing that can help sell the pitch is the back story. "You want to develop the story behind the book," Rosenblum said. "If it's a novel, it could be what inspired you to write it. If it's a nonfiction narrative, it's what evidence you have to create it; there are so many pitches out there. You have to cut through that noise. I know we talk about platform, but you have to find a way so your voice comes out of the book and be an advocate for it."

Ebook metadata, Friedman says, is also a key component to marketing your book. Friedman describes metadata as all the stuff you would see if you actually picked up a book in the bookstore, plus a little more. So, the cover, the book blurb, the sample pages and, on Amazon, keywords and categories. This metadata will flesh out the book for readers who are seeking out that information, so they can find it and purchase it. "Good metadata increases sales," Friedman said. "I heard a talk from someone who specializes in this and they said, the biggest kiss of death for any book is to be categorized as fiction general."

While free is controversial in the author community, Friedman recommended free as a marketing strategy. "For an unknown author, you need to make your book generally cheap or possibly free," she said. "That's how it works. Who plays Candy Crush? It's free to start, but you have to pay 99 cent to go to the next level. You need to pay 99 cents if you're going to get the hammer. The basic concept is loyalty comes first and you monetize later." She noted that a popular and effective trend for series is to make the first one permanently free and charge a higher price for the remaining books in the series.

Friedman said authors should also create content (beside the book) that connects with their readers. "I call it thinking beyond the book," Friedman said. "We have to think about content in ways that go beyond the book's covers. So, there is no hard-and-fast rule. You don't have to have a movie or a podcast, but you have to think about what things broaden the content. It's really an act of your imagination. What would readers genuinely delight in if you created it?"

Finally, sticking around may be an author's greatest marketing tool. "Authors have found a book's profitability doesn't stop after the first three months it is on sale," Friedman said. "You'll always have new people interested in going back to your backlist."

http://www.indiesunlimited.com/2014/03/31/book-festival-experts-offer-advice-on-building-author-platform/

How to Create Book Club Questions for your Novel
Posted on February 18, 2014 by RJ Crayton

As authors, we want our books read, and what better place than at book clubs? So, if your book is chosen by a book club, one thing you can do to make it easy for the group (besides writing a great book) is give them questions.

Many books published nowadays come with a series of "Book Club" or "Discussion" questions at the end. So, how do you create these questions for your book?

First, you'll want to familiarize yourself with book club questions. There are sites (like this one[56] and this one[57]) that offer questions that can be used with any book. That's good for getting a feel of what to ask. Also, you'll want to look at questions for popular books in your genre. Simply Google "book club questions for (TITLE)." If the publisher created questions for the book, you should get a hit.

Now that you have a feel for the types of questions asked, move on to your novel. Book club questions tend to evaluate themes, characters, and relationships, so you'll want to note the major themes, characters, and relationships in your book, so you can create questions that touch on them. One tricky part with creating questions is that they sometimes include spoilers. Because a potential reader might stumble upon them, or an actual reader might glance at them midway through the book, it's usually limited to minor spoilage. (This is the only instance where minor spoilage is OK. If someone tells you the tuna salad has suffered minor spoilage, don't eat it.)

Here's a publisher provided book club question for the *The Help*: "Do you think that had Aibileen stayed working for Miss Elizabeth, that Mae Mobley would have grown up to be racist like her mother?" This question clearly lets people know that Aibileen didn't work for Miss Elizabeth for the duration of the book. But it's not such a huge spoiler that someone who glances at the questions says, "Darn, now the entire book is ruined." The thing with spoilers is to provide the

---

[56] Sample book club questions, https://www.bookbrowse.com/bookclubs/advice/index.cfm/fuseaction/diy_guides?

[57] Sample book club questions, http://www.bookbundlz.com/BBArticle.aspx?articleId=25

minimum information necessary for the reader to understand what issue from the book you want to explore with the question.

Now that you understand what's needed, you can start writing questions relevant to your book. Remember, questions should be open ended so they spur discussion. You can ask things like: Why was the color red so important to the character of Strawberry? How do you think Hansel's childhood trauma in the forest impacted his all-consuming desire to be the world's best map maker? What was the significance of Ariel devouring a crab cake in front of her friend Sebastian?

If you want to have really great questions, use reader feedback to craft them. There are multiple ways to do this. You can ask readers which parts of the books they felt most passionate about. If your book is already published, you may be able to glean some feedback from reading reviews. With either method, if the issue keeps coming up (readers tell you it's the thing that they loved or hated most), it probably will make great fodder for a question.

Another thing you can do is host (or attend) a book club meeting for your book. Grab some readers (or beta readers, if unpublished) and discuss the book in a comfy setting. The book club I belong to read my book, and the feedback was enlightening, as people had thoughts that just hadn't occurred to me. Toward the end of the discussion, one person said, "Wow, Susan was some friend, 'cause I can't think of a single friend I would do that for." For me, Susan's choice in the book was one that was so inherently who she was and so inherently representative of those characters' friendship, that I never really considered her choice from an outside point of view. The discussion over this issue was passionate (big clue in that others might feel this way, too). After the meeting, I used that notion to create one of my book club questions[58]. So, reader feedback can lead you to lively questions.

Once you've written your book club questions, include them at the back of your book. If you've done the questions prepublication, great. If your book is already published, add the questions to your website, and write a blog post mentioning you now have questions for book clubs. Update any editions of the book you can easily change (this should include all ebook editions; and possibly your print edition).

http://www.indiesunlimited.com/2014/02/18/how-to-create-book-club-questions-for-your-novel/

---

[58] RJ Crayton's Book Club Questions for Life First, http://rjcrayton.com/books/life-first/book-club-questions-life-first-2/

Legal issues for authors: from copyright to contracts
May 21, 2013

On Saturday, I attended a brief workshop on legal issues for writers, sponsored by CityLit and the Maryland Volunteer Lawyers for the Arts (MDVLA). The speakers were Cynthia Sanders, president of MDVLA, and, agent/attorney, Laura Strachan.

Here are some of the highlights of the informative presentation/discussion:

- **If you use copyrighted material in your work**, you need permission or you have to pay licensing fees. This is particularly important if you're doing nonfiction, and you want to use letters from people. For any kinds of work — fiction or nonfiction — song lyrics and excerpts from other works of fiction require you to get permission. Strachan noted that most major book publishers have a "Permissions" department, and it just takes finding them to request permission to excerpt their work in your work. For smaller publishers that may not have a "permissions" department, be persistent. You may have to call a few people. Sanders notes that some people will "say no just because don't want to have to hire a lawyer to figure it out." For song lyrics, see the next bullet point. Letters from someone to you (which might be used in a memoir) will require permission from the letter writer, who holds the copyright.
- **Song lyrics are a pain in the butt.** Clearly I'm paraphrasing here, but song lyrics are copyrighted works, and the musicians who wrote them tend to want to get paid if you use them. Both Sanders and Strachan agreed it's often hard to find who the rights holders are (artist, a publishing company, record label) and it's expensive to get them. So, the simplest advice is to not use them. It's generally OK to use an occasional song title in the main text of your books (example: in the middle of a paragraph, you write: "Jane's favorite album was the Beatles' Abbey Road"). However, you could get into copyright issues if you try to use song titles as the title of your book or as headers or chapter titles. Then, it's as if you're trading on the song's good name to support your work.
- **Fair use can be complicated.** There is the doctrine of fair

use, that allows you to use small portions of copyrighted material without needing permission of the owner or to pay a licensing fee. This is done for the benefit of public discourse and is strongest when you're using it in noncommercial uses (such as teaching). For commercial uses, it can get kind of complicated. For example, generally when you use only a small portion of the work in your piece, you might be able to argue fair use. But, that's not true with song lyrics. With parody, you have to use enough of the work's character and substance for people to recognize the original work and know it's a parody. But, a parody also has to be making fun of the original work. A group that tried to use the Cat in the Hat to make fun of something other than the book the Cat in the Hat lost their parody claim. At that point, it became licensing. So, it's tricky business. More on Fair Use is online at http://www.copyright.gov/fls/fl102.html.

- **Memoir writers, you need permission.** Apparently, people are entitled to a right to privacy. So, if you're writing a memoir that exposes your exes philandering, you need to get your exes permission before publishing. 'What-the-what?' You say! Yes, this surprised me, too. I always think of celebrity tell-alls and the juicy gossip they unearth. But, the lawyers mentioned that celebrities have less right to privacy. Your average man on the street is entitled to some privacy and they can sue you if you violate it by airing their dirty secrets in your memoir. Strachan noted that most publishers ask you to get consent agreements from people mentioned. And some publishers require you to get something known as E&O (errors and omissions) insurance, to insure you against lawsuits from angry people mentioned in your book. The lawyers mentioned E&O was more common with nonfiction and film productions.

- **All contracts are negotiable.** "If someone has taken the time to create a contract for you, they're willing to negotiate," Strachan said. So, don't feel rushed to sign on the dotted line.

- **Always know what rights you're assigning in a contract.** According to the lawyers, there are all sorts of rights to your work that you could give up or assign during a contract. Some of these include first printing permission, English language rights and world rights. If you're not careful, you could end up signing a contract that precludes you from writing a sequel to your own book. Also, they say it's important to know when your rights revert to you. It used to be that authors got their rights back when a book went out of print, but with digital publishing, that could be never. So do know what you're signing.

- **Published work should have a registered copyright.** The lawyers agreed that in traditional book publishing, if you're sending to agents, you don't need to register a copyright for that work. It's likely to get changed before the final publication. However, once your work is to the point of publication, it needs a registered copyright. If you are self-publishing, you should register your copyright (file electronically and get your registration number; the certificate won't come for months, but once you have your number you're good to go). Any traditional publisher will take care of copyright registration prior to publishing as well. A registered copyright shifts the burden of proof to the infringer, and allows you to get statutory damages for each infringing act (statutory damages means there is a set amount of money written into law that you are entitled to if someone has violated your copyright; without statutory damages, you have to prove how much money they made off your work and get actual damages, which is quite difficult).

- **Public Domain Works.** I probably could have put this after permissions, but it's late and I'm not thinking clearly (writing at 1 am, and set it to publish later today). If you want to quote from an older work—one that is public domain—you don't need permission. Sometimes public domain works are reworked (the Wizard of Oz is public domain; The Wiz is not), so be sure you're using the public domain work.

- **Legal help is available.** This was the coolest thing I learned from the workshop: MDVLA has lawyers available to help. They'll review a contract by appointment, or otherwise help out low-income artists. How cool is that? Check out their website for more info: http://mdvla.org.

http://rjcrayton.com/2013/05/21/legal-issues-for-authors-from-copyright-to-contracts/

When Your Books Outlive You — Estate Planning Experts Offer Advice for Writers
Posted on January 26, 2015 by RJ Crayton

So, you've built a writing empire, or more likely, you've published a couple of books and they sell enough to pay your cable bill each month (or your coffee bill, if on a smaller scale). Now, you die; what happens? Well, that is going to depend on how you've planned for it. I talked to a couple of estate planning experts on what self-published writers need to do to ensure their intellectual property assets (that fancy legal term for your books) pass on in a way that you want. Estate planning, like a good novel, has a few twists and turns, so here's the skinny so you don't get caught off guard.

Our First Twist: You May Not Die Immediately
Chad Whitfield, an attorney with Hunter, Smith and Davis in Tennessee, says most people don't just die. More often people are incapacitated first, perhaps by a long illness or a tragic accident. If you are incapacitated, you need a durable power of attorney. That document will allow the person you appoint to access your financial accounts and make health decisions (depending on the nature of the power of attorney document) while you are incapacitated. Unless you have a durable power of attorney, your spouse (or other closest relative) won't be able to access any account they're not listed on, without going to court first.

"In most states, if you're over 18 and become incapacitated and don't have a power of attorney, the court has to appoint a conservatorship," Whitfield said. "That can take months and cost thousands of dollars." In general, the court will appoint a spouse or family member as conservator, but it requires a hearing to make sure the appointed person will act in your best interests, and you have to pay the court fees that accompany that hearing.

So rather than waste time and money in court, Whitfield recommends getting the durable power of attorney, which lasts until you revoke it. This is good in one sense, because you do it once and move on. However, if your circumstances change — such as a divorce, or the person you name predeceases you, or you just now hate the person's guts — you need to revoke the document and create a new one. "I encourage my clients to, every two or three years, pull out the documents and review them — see if they need to change anything."

No More Surprises: You're Dead

So, your illness has ended and now you're dead. What happens to your IP assets? Same thing as all your other assets. If you died without a will, you die intestate. That means, the state will decide how your assets are distributed.

"There are 50 states and each of the 50 states has its own intestacy rules," says Julian Block, an attorney and author based in Larchmont, N.Y. "What the intestacy rules do is spell out who gets your property in the event of your death without a will. In a lot of states, it's 50 percent to a surviving spouse and the remainder divided among the children. If there's no surviving spouse, then divided among the children. If no children, look to the grandparents."

Because intestacy rules are not specific to your situation, Block notes that dying without a will, "could result in some, or a lot, of your property going to a person or individuals you never intended to see your property go to — perhaps individuals you loathe."

If you don't want your state's intestacy laws to decide what happens to your IP, then you need, at a minimum, a will. If you want a say in managing how your IP is handled after you die, you probably want a trust or something more elaborate, like an LLC.

Keeping it Simple

The simplest way to deal with your IP assets is to will them to who you would like and provide a "letter of instruction," says Block. The will is the legal document that determines who your assets are transferred to after your death. The "letter of instruction" is a non-legal document that offers guidance for your heirs on closing your estate, and your wishes.

"The main goal of a letter of instruction is to let your heirs know what you have and what your preferences might be," Block said. "In context of writers, your heirs need to know, 'do you have money coming to you?'"

If you're a hybrid author and have some contracts with publishing houses, your heirs need to know which houses you're at and what you have due. For all your self-published titles, your heirs need to know where your accounts are. Block recommends creating a list of all the places you've published your books using direct accounts, such as Amazon.com, Nookpress (for Barnes and Noble), Apple, Libiro, and All Romance ebooks. If you used a distributor, such as Smashwords or

Draft2Digital, list which retailers you chose to distribute your book to via that distributor. (It should be accurate; if your family is going to monitor/close out accounts, they'll need to know they've gotten everything).

"The letter of final instructions needs to include where I have my bank accounts and my brokerage accounts," he notes. Given that most accounts are electronic, it's unlikely heirs will find your accounts unless you specifically list them. If your book royalties get paid to a separate bank account, you should ensure your heirs know what that bank is.

You can list the assets and accounts as an attached page, as the letter of final instruction might also include things like funeral arrangements (whether you wish to be buried, cremated, or donated to science). Your asset list should include enough information for the person to find the account, so you may want to include account numbers. If you do, keep the list in a secure location to avoid issues with improper access to your accounts while you're alive. Whitfield says many of his clients purchase a small safe and share the code with select family members. While you want the list in a secure location, documents that a person needs to close your estate, such as an asset list, should not be kept a safe deposit box at a bank. Both Whitfield and Block noted it may take weeks to get into a bank safe deposit box after a person dies.

When planning for your IP assets after your death, also consider what you want done with your unfinished works. "You've got this magnum opus you've been working on for years," Block said. "If it's unfinished at the time of your death and you do want it completed, you could say, 'I have some candidates that can finish the job.' However, another school of thought is to say, 'If it's not complete at my death, I don't want it touched. Forget about it.'" Whatever you want done, it should be made clear in writing.

While a will controls what happens to many assets, some assets have built-in controls. For example, bank accounts and retirement accounts ask for a "pay on death" beneficiary. "People need to make sure the beneficiaries read how they want them to read," Whitfield noted. This often comes up in divorce situations, where an ex-spouse is the beneficiary of an account. If your book royalties go to a separate bank account, be sure the beneficiary is correct.

While a will is a great way for writers to determine what happens to their assets after their death, it does have some drawbacks. One is that the will disposes of the assets once and then it has no more control. If

you leave your books rights to your spouse, who is also the other bio-
logical parent of your children, that's great. But, then if your spouse
remarries, and dies, leaving your book rights to a new spouse, your
children could end up with nothing, while a stranger enjoys the profits
from your books. Writers who want more control over what happens
to their IP assets after death may want to consider a trust. Unfortunately, we're running long as is, so on Friday we'll talk about the advantages of a trust or an LLC for writers, as both allow the entity (trust
or LLC) to own book rights, passing on the income to a spouse or
child.

Part II — A Trust or an LLC Can Help Manage Author Assets after Death
Posted on January 30, 2015 by RJ Crayton

Yay, you came back! On Monday, we talked about what happens to a writer's intellectual property (IP) after they die. A will was mentioned as a fairly simple way to pass on this asset. However, a will has some drawbacks.

"Every state is different, but a will can spend up to a year in probate," said Chad, an attorney with Hunter, Smith and Davis in Tennessee. "It has to stay open between four months and a year, and things become public. The copyrights you own, all the assets have to be on the inventory. Some people like to keep it private. With a living trust, you can accomplish the same goals, but it's private."

The other issue with an income-generating item is if you leave something to a person via a will, it is theirs to do with as they please. "Most of the time it will go to the kids outright and they can fight over it, or sell the rights," Whitfield said. "If I want the kids to get the benefit of it, but not own it, then that has to have proactive planning."

One way to do that is with a trust, which is essentially a legal entity that acts as a bucket to hold your assets and is governed by a set of instructions (the trust document). The trust gives the "trustee" latitude to make decisions that fulfill your instructions.

"[Clients will] create a trust that owns the copyright interests and they'll have a third party be the trustee that oversees it," Whitfield said.

When a trust owns the IP asset, the trustee can make decisions to manage it, and pay out the royalties to the beneficiaries. If the trust, rather than a person owns the asset, it insulates the asset from liability. "Let's say a book takes off and the book goes to a kid whose marriage does not last," Whitfield said. "If it's in a trust for the kids, it's protected. It's not an asset that needs to be divided in the divorce. [Or] if the kids are physicians or in a high risk business, where they can get sued, being in the trust will protect those assets."

So, how long can your assets be managed in the trust? Each state's law is different, but probably long enough to cover the time period covered by copyright (the life of the author + 70 years[59]). "In Tennessee, you can have a trust in place for 300 years," Whitfield said.

---

[59] Copyright duration, http://www.copyright.gov/title17/92chap3.html#302

In addition to having some control over what happens with the asset after death, there's also another advantage to a living trust. "The living trust is a private document and it's harder to challenge," Whitfield said. "The timeframe to challenge a will is two years, whereas a living trust is 90 days."

If you establish a trust, you'll need to give some thought as to who will be the trustee after your death. That person should understand your writing, and be able to oversee all the royalty streams and handle any issues that arise with the books. One last note about trusts: A living trust is revocable and is used when the author is alive. Revocable trusts offer no protection against lawsuits, as the living trust is the same as a person. With a living (revocable) trust, the author is the trustee during his or her lifetime. A successor trustee takes over after the author's death, at which time the trust converts to an irrevocable trust (the kind that offers protection against lawsuits). If you place your assets in the trust while you are living, when you die, your assets will pass privately to heirs. If you don't put your assets in the trust while you are living and simply will them to the trust, the assets will go through probate, like any other willed assets.

Make Lovers, Not Fighters

A death is a difficult and stressful time for survivors due to the loss, but fights over assets can make it more difficult. Both Whitfield and, attorney, Julian Block say that minimizing fighting amongst heirs is a worthy goal in estate planning.

If you're one of those types who says, "I'm dead and gone, what do I care if the kids fight," Whitfield has something for you to consider. "Do you want me to make more money?" He asks with a laugh. If the kids decide to make a court challenge, then the estate has to deal with that in court, and the money to pay the legal fees to defend the challenge comes from the estate. "It's always the lawyers who make the money out of it. So, do you want me or your kids to have the money?"

What are the common issues people fight over? Well, the heart of it is money, but the cause of the fight is really failed expectations, the lawyers contend. Julian Block said it's important for people to talk to their heirs about what they plan to do so the reality meets their expectations.

"It's less likely there will be a family squabble if it's been discussed," Block said. "If your intention is to leave everything to your son and daughter, then have a meeting with your son and daughter. The main point is to plan ahead and anticipate what is going to come up."

Be honest not just with your heirs but with your attorney, as he or she can often make suggestions that will help you create harmony and carry out your wishes. "You need to be bluntly honest with your attorney," Whitfield said. "Don't tell your attorney you have three kids and they get along just fine, if they don't."

Simple things can cause conflict. "If they have more than one child, they have to decide which one they want to appoint as executor," Whitfield said. "Sometimes there's mistrust there [among siblings] and you may want to appoint a bank or third party. Be honest about the way the children are, and we can make suggestions to head off problems."

The Remainders

We covered most of the issues above, but I'll throw in a couple here at the bottom that Block and Whitfield noted.

While wills and trusts are great, Whitfield notes that writers also have the option of setting up an LLC (limited liability corporation) to manage their writing IP. This is mainly done to avoid your writing assets being attacked in a lawsuit. The LLC, because it's a corporation, also transitions nicely after your death, because it's got a definitive structure for managing the assets.

An LLC, however, is a more complicated legal structure with managers and managing members, and it's probably not necessary for most writers, as it's expensive to maintain if you don't have much writing income. "I can't quote for all lawyers, but in Tennessee, you're going to spend a $300 annual fee to the state and $12 to record it," Whitfield said. "And you're going to have a one-time fee to a lawyer to set it up, of $800 to $1200."

Block cautioned that heirs should get proper tax advice for royalty income they receive from your books. "As a writer, you receive book royalties," Block said. "You are liable for income taxes. You are liable for self-employment tax. But, after you die, if your daughter receives royalties, she is liable for income tax just like you are. She is not obligated to pay the self-employment taxes. She didn't do the work, so she's like someone who is getting royalties from a mine or oil well."

For those who are gung ho to create or amend their wills, Legal

Zoom notes the cost of a will [60] through an attorney ranges from $150-$600, while the cost of a will along with trust documents can run from $1,000 to $1,500.

[60] Legal Zoom on the cost of a will, http://info.legalzoom.com/average-cost-making-20354.html

THANK YOU

Thank you for purchasing this book. I really hope it helps you in your self-publishing journey. If you've found the information at all useful, I'd love it if you left a review of the book on Amazon and Goodreads.

Amazon Page
http://www.amazon.com/dp/B00SSK3G14

Goodreads Page
https://www.goodreads.com/book/show/24852349-the-self-publishing-road-map

Join the Mailing List. Would you like to get updates about my new books or a chance to win Advanced Review Copies or freebies? If so, join my mailing list. Go to the subscribe page, http://www.rjcrayton.com/subscribe, and supply your email address. That's it. We never spam you or sell your email address.

ABOUT THE AUTHOR

R.J. Crayton grew up in Illinois and now lives in the Maryland suburbs of Washington, DC. She is the author of the *Life First* series of novels, which includes *Life First, Second Life* and *Third Life: Taken*. Prior to writing fiction, Crayton was a journalist, writing for newspapers, including the *Wichita Eagle* and *Kansas City Star*. Crayton also worked for several trade publications, including *Solid Waste Report, Education Technology News*, and *Campus Crime*. In addition to her novels, Crayton published *Four Mothers*, a short story collection, in 2014. Crayton is a monthly contributor to the Indies Unlimited blog and a regular contributor to the Institute for Ethics and Emerging Technologies blog. When she's not writing, Crayton spends her time being a ninja mom (stealthy and ultra cool, like moms should be) to her son and daughter. You can find out more about her at http://rjcrayton.com.

R.J. Crayton loves connecting with readers. If you talk to her, she'll talk back, so please check her out at the following places:

Website
http://rjcrayton.com

Facebook
https://www.facebook.com/rjcraytonauthor

Twitter
https://twitter.com/RJCrayton

Goodreads
http://www.goodreads.com/author/show/7111348.R_J_Crayton

Pinterest
http://www.pinterest.com/rjcrayton

ALSO BY THIS AUTHOR

Life First

"I was completely intrigued by this book from the very first page. There were fairly few characters in-keeping with the story, but they were all extremely well thought out. I really think RJ Crayton should be expecting calls for film rights because this played out in my mind as I read it like a really great film.... It gripped you like King Kong and would not let go until you had finished the book."
- BestChickLit.com

Strong-willed Kelsey Reed must escape tonight or tomorrow her government will take her kidney and give it to someone else.

In this future forged by survivors of pandemics that wiped out 80 percent of the world's population, life is valued above all else. The mentally ill are sterilized, abortions are illegal and those who refuse to donate an organ when told are sentenced to death.

Determined not to give up her kidney or die, Kelsey enlists the help of her boyfriend Luke and a dodgy doctor to escape. The trio must disable the tracking chip in her arm for her to flee undetected. If they fail, Kelsey will be stripped of everything.

: http://www.amazon.com/dp/B00DFNWFX4 .

Second Life

"Twists and turns with a dash or two of betrayal."
-Amazon Reviewer

"I just cant give the twists away, but you will be sat on the edge of your seat."
-Amazon Reviewer

Susan Harper is being held captive by her government. As the normally feisty Susan's hopes of freedom dwindle, a mysterious stranger sneaks into her room and promises to help.

Susan and mystery man Rob grow close as he tries to orchestrate her escape. When the duo discovers the truth behind Susan's captivity, they realize they must act quickly if they're to save her. Susan and Rob will need more than passion for each other and their wits to succeed. They will need help from old friends, including Kelsey Reed.

In the previous book, Life First, Susan gave Kelsey a chance at a second life. But now will she get her own?

Amazon Page: http://www.amazon.com/dp/B00H314SOS

Third Life: Taken

"This was the best book of the series and the perfect conclusion to the story. It was a stomach churning, tension filled rollercoaster of emotions as you followed the two distinct but intertwined plots."
-Chuckles Book Cave

When Kelsey Reed fled her country to escape a forced kidney transplant, she was sure she'd never return. However, when her brother-in-law shows up on her doorstep, he commits an act of betrayal that changes everything.

Forced to head back to the nation that tried to kill her, Kelsey will need the help of her husband Luke, and friends Susan and Rob to escape with her life.

Amazon Page: http://www.amazon.com/dp/B00NG63ZKC

Four Mothers

Sometimes, a mother's flaws are dangerous...

Four stories. Four mothers. Four crises. One great read.

Our notions of motherhood run the gamut from the mythical SuperMom to the dreaded Mommy Dearest. None is entirely true, as all mothers are both perfect and flawed. Four mothers tells four stories of mothers who each face a crises, either real or perceived, in their parenting life. *Change the way you see motherhood.*

In *Almost Perfect*, we see our Mommy Dearest end of the spectrum with Bitsy. She wants her grandson, whom she is raising to be perfect, and with Bitsy, we are reminded, it's not just stepmothers who are wicked. (Note: You can now read *Almost Perfect* as a FREE standalone short story: http://www.amazon.com/dp/B00USBHSAG)

Tilda, the mother we meet in *As Luck Would Have It*, exudes luck from every pore. She would love to be the super mom who saves the day for her family, but she has one problem - her daughter's seeming lack of luck. In fact, Tilda's luck fails whenever her daughter is around. Tilda's solution to this problem could prove problematic.

Felicity is relishing her overbearing husband's absence on a business trip, when her *Two-Day Break* suddenly turns into a nightmare.

In *The Beads*, Iram is a mother coping with crisis — a child in a coma after nearly choking to death — when something happens that affects her entire outlook.

Also included in the collection is a bonus story, *Lynch Party*, about a mother who has a different perspective on what makes a great party activity.

Amazon Page: http://www.amazon.com/dp/B00KWMLOOM